D1499602

Beer Hunter, Whisky Chaser

Beer Hunter, Whisky Chaser

CONTRIBUTIONS BY

Stephen Beaumont

Julie Bradford

Dave Broom

Ian Buxton

John Hansell

Charles MacLean

Hans Offringa

F Paul Pacult

Roger Protz

Lucy Saunders

Conrad Seidl

Gavin D Smith

AND

Carolyn Smagalski

EDITED BY

Ian Buxton

Parkinson's
Disease Society

Classic Expressions
www.classicexpressions.co.uk

First published by
Classic Expressions
an imprint of
Distilled Discourse Ltd
Distillery House
Tomdachoille
by Pitlochry
PH16 5NA
www.classicexpressions.co.uk

The profits of the sales of this book will be
donated to the Parkinson's Disease Society (UK).

Distilled Discourse Ltd gratefully acknowledges support
given to the production of this work by The Glenlivet.

A catalogue record of this book is
available from the British Library.

ISBN: 978-1-906000-04-2

First published in March 2009

Designed by Mark Blackadder

Cover design by Gill Allan, Mercat Design

Printed and bound in Poland

CONTENTS

INTRODUCTION

Ian Buxton

De mortuis nil nisi bonum dicendum est.

Chilon of Sparta

The news of Michael Jackson's untimely death spread rapidly through the worlds of whisky and beer. Amongst those who knew him there was a sense of shock, but scarcely of surprise: his illness, borne with stoic dignity for so long, had visibly progressed. The deterioration of his health was painfully obvious and, on several occasions prior to his death, he had seemed gravely ill.

I first met Michael in February 1984 when we spent a week touring Czech breweries. For more than 20 years we met intermittently at whisky events – conferences, tastings and distillery and industry functions. Our last encounter was memorable even before its significance became clear. In the course of a long conversation at Craigellachie's Highlander Inn during the 2007 Speyside Whisky Festival, he chose to reminisce about that trip behind the Iron Curtain, recalling with astonishing clarity incidents and fellow travellers that I had long forgotten. Later he spoke of moving to the United States; of making 'a fresh start' – from what, I could not discern.

In retrospect, it was a curious conversation: typical of Michael in its elliptical form, rambling, diffuse but warm and deeply humane, always illuminated by his abiding interest in people and his restless curiosity. Yet even at the time it struck me as having an elegiac quality and afterwards I was vaguely troubled by his apparently effortless recall of distant, trivial events.

So news of his death was a shock, but not a surprise. Within

1

an hour the plan for this book had formed, yet I did not act for some while on the initial impulse. There were others more qualified, I reasoned, others who knew Michael better, others with greater resources. I knew also that there would be other plans: a Memorial Service, perhaps, and commemorative bottling of his favourite beers or whiskies. It seemed crass and, even in some ill-defined way, opportunistic to push the merits of this modest proposal.

But though other projects crowded forward I remained convinced that something permanent was required. A Memorial Service is ephemeral and reaches only a limited audience, however satisfying for the participants (and I do not mean to decry its importance). By its very nature it excludes many and the memory of it inevitably fades with time. So too, with the finest of commemorative bottles (and again I applaud the initiative): once opened and drunk their glories are fleeting and transitory, yet Michael would hardly have welcomed them becoming mere trophies for collectors.

And Michael was not a brewer or distiller. He was a journalist and writer. Above all, what he stood for and cared about, even more passionately than rugby league or jazz or, yes, whisky or beer (and he cared deeply about these fine and worthy things) was honest writing.

So it seemed most appropriate to remember him with words. But not, I reasoned, a collection of personal essays on what Michael meant to various luminaries. This seemed to me likely to pall very rapidly, to become repetitive and, possibly a worse horror for a Yorkshireman, to descend into the sentimental and maudlin. Moreover, anyone buying this book would, in all probability, have their own memories of Michael Jackson, their own stories, their own tributes. Yet, whatever their merit or personal significance, not all of these stories can be told whilst the process of selection itself seemed to me demeaning, implying greater worth or interest in one memory over another.

What is more, given the inevitable delay in compiling, editing and printing a volume such as this, it seemed better to honour his name by looking forward rather than with recollection. The time for obituaries is now past, I argued, and those who walk in Michael's shadow should attempt something that would have engaged and intrigued him, not simply an exercise in self-indulgent and morbid flattery. Let us honour Michael with *words*, fresh and new writing on beer and whisky that he would have enjoyed reading; that he would have respected; that he might even have wished to have written himself.

Or so I argued to a small group of other beer and whisky writers. And, to my considerable surprise and even more considerable pleasure, it seemed they agreed. I determined that this collection of essays should be evenly balanced: six of the best writers on each subject would be recruited to contribute a new essay, on a subject of their choosing.

I made only two stipulations: there were to be no personal reminiscences or anecdotes about Michael, for the reasons outlined above; and the material was to be new. And a third, final but critical thing: the author was to be *proud* of what they had written. (Oh, and there was no fee!).

My initial enquiries were, I hope, both tentative and modest (I hope the authors would collectively agree) yet with each response I grew in confidence and belief, for I did not receive one refusal. Acceptance was in every case immediate and full-blooded – with 12 emails or phone calls I solicited contributions from 12 internationally renowned authors, several of whom I had never met (and indeed have still to meet).

Lest I sound vain I should add that this is nothing to do with me. It is the finest and most heartfelt tribute to Michael Jackson that his peers could make. I was merely the lightning rod for their passionate need to express their respect, admiration and loss in a way that seemed both more appropriate and more profoundly felt than any tribute or valediction.

I should properly add here that, when word of the project belatedly spread amongst the community of drinks writers, the size of this volume could easily have doubled. Perhaps in a future edition that will be possible but, with publication deadlines to meet, a decision had to be made simply in order to get this into print. So, if your favourite whisky or beer writer does not appear in these pages the fact is that they probably wanted to be here and I either neglected to approach them (I was initially reticent to ask fellow professionals to contribute their work for nothing) or simply misunderstood the depth of feeling that I could have tapped.

What you hold in your hands, then, poor thing though it may be, is testament to Michael from at least some of those best placed to value and appreciate what he achieved. Michael was not the first writer on either beer or whisky; arguably, he was not the finest, but he was indisputably the most influential. For that he will be long remembered and it is to acknowledge the remarkable achievement of his life and work that this collection of essays has been compiled.

If variety is what you celebrate in your choice of whisky or beer, then this is truly a joyous and eclectic celebration of a life well-lived. Amongst these pages you will find both fact and fiction. In no particular order, John Hansell has contributed a very poignant private memoir and both F Paul Pacult and Dave Broom have elected to tell us something about their personal, and very different, journeys into whisky. Hans Offringa's contribution is a short story, though you may feel that you recognise the character of Alan MacManus.

Stephen Beaumont has taken a more scientific approach, discussing the impact of environment and context on beer drinking, whilst Gavin D Smith (better known, perhaps, as a whisky writer but very well qualified to expound on beer) investigates 30 years of British beer which roughly matches the period of Michael Jackson's contribution on the subject. This is mirrored by Julie Johnson's review of the last three decades of American brewing and an authoritative analysis of the development of single malt whisky by Charles MacLean.

Conrad Seidl goes in search of German beer culture and well-known British beer writer Roger Protz discusses lagering. Lucy Saunders offers a practical guide to beer and food and in my essay I have sought to discuss the problem of 'authenticity' and what it means for Scotch whisky.

But this volume could not be complete without some

personal reminiscence of Michael, and no one is better suited to that task than his partner, Carolyn Smagalski, who writes movingly of the Michael she knew. Apart from this introduction and Carolyn's contribution, the other essays are organised in alphabetical order of the authors' surnames.

In editing this volume I have tried to take a light touch. All the contributors are experienced and widely published and it seemed impertinent to make any significant alteration to their work. All spellings, however, have been standardised to reflect English usage ('flavour' for 'flavor,' for example) except where the context makes it clear that the American variant is required. Hence alternate spellings of 'whisky' and 'whiskey' are not errors but reflect an individual author's predilection for Scotch or Bourbon respectively.

All of the writers, and Gill Allan our jacket designer, contributed their work free of charge and we have received generous sponsorship from Chivas Brothers' The Glenlivet to offset the cost of production. My colleague Neil Wilson at Classic Expressions took on the onerous responsibility of publisher with considerable grace, especially considering that I 'volunteered' him for this role.

To all of them go my thanks and the gratitude of the Parkinson's Disease Society of the UK. Michael suffered from the debilitating effects of this dreadful disease with grace and true Yorkshire grit for many years. It is fitting, then, that all profits from the publication of this book will be donated to the Parkinson's Disease Society of the UK. To this end, I add particular thanks to you, the purchaser, for buying this book. You may never see the good that this has done, but it is appreciated and valued more than you can know.

Whatever your tipple, savour it with the knowledge that Michael Jackson is by your side – a reliable, robust and modest guide whose memory and influence lives on.

Slainte!
Ian Buxton

CHAPTER ONE
QUINTESSENTIALLY MICHAEL

Carolyn Smagalski

First impressions so deeply root in our psyche that neither place nor time can diminish them. 'The Jura Scholar,' 'Doctor of Drams,' 'Professor of the Pint.' Humble, yet arrogant. Rumpled, yet royal. A bit off balance. Gracious in manner and prescient in wisdom.

Michael Jackson belonged to us. We, who quaffed the dram and the pint, laid claim to our treasure and to his digressions. Had he come from Oxford or Yale, he may have been less accessible, but we embraced this champion of the working class. His tongue titillated our own with tales of international flavours – sour lambic from the valley of the Zenne in Belgium, single malt from the Isle of Islay, and imperial stout from the Baltic nations of Europe. He called himself the 'Beer Hunter' and the 'Whisky Chaser.' With deadpan wit, he introduced Golden Shower Imperial Pilsner to NBC chat-show host Conan O'Brien with the cunning innocence of a fox. We understood his subtleties and he became our rock star.

What drove us to such lustful thirst?

Jackson was a man's man, irascible in the face of competition. His tempestuous nature sharpened at the sweat-drenched jab of a boxer's glove or the oncoming crush of a bloodstained scrum of rugby league ... not union ... league. Jackson's own native Huddersfield in West Yorkshire spawned 26 newspapers by the late 1950s. This was the golden age. The air, awash with solvents that burned the eyes and seared the throat, inspired a hunger for newsprint within this industrial town. Local pubs, thick with the smell of blood pudding and booze, held cynicism between their teeth, stoked with the ever-present scintillation of a story about to crack. This was where he *belonged*. At 16, Jackson initiated a series called 'This is your Pub' through the *Batley & Morley Gazette*. With notebook in hand, he would work the weekly papers in Mirfield and Wakefield before landing a professional position with the daily *Huddersfield Examiner*, and eventually, Fleet Street in London.

Jackson amassed a personal collection of mentors, both in the physical sense and in his mental reserves: Dylan Thomas and his autobiographical tale *Old Garbo* from *Portrait of the Artist as a Young Dog*; Faulkner, Joyce, Burns and Hemingway; William Empson's *Seven Types of Ambiguity* and Bruce Chatwin's telegraphic words 'Have gone to Patagonia' that scorched *The Sunday Times* in 1974. Clearly, there was a common thread shared by all – drink. This one key was worth keeping.

On assignment, from sexploitation in Amsterdam to civil war in Bangladesh, Jackson sustained a 20-year foreplay with intoxications that soothed the soul and loosened the tongue. As a documentarian, he had yet to assemble a serious journal as a drinks writer. Beer sustained every civilisation in the world, with whisky close at heel. Why, then, were these not celebrated with the enthusiasm of champagne?

By 1976, Michael Jackson introduced himself to the drinks community with his book, *The English Pub*. It was but a small introduction, a whisper in a field of grain. With his 1977 release of *The World Guide to Beer*, however, he captivated a global community with his words, 'A man who doesn't care about the beer he drinks may as well not care about the bread he eats. Beer may have been man's staple diet before bread was invented, and these two staffs of life are as comparable as they are closely related.' It would be another ten years before he would sate aficionados of single malts and blends with *Michael Jackson's World Guide to Whisky*.

Wild fermentation in Wallonia and Flanders neared extinction until Jackson's 1991 book, *Great Beers of Belgium*, followed by the enormously celebrated 'The Burgundies of Belgium,' a sobriquet used in his video-tape series *The Beer*

Hunter. In 1994, he was honoured by Crown Prince Philippe of Belgium with the Mercurius Award.

A foodie by nature, Jackson celebrated each new experience, whether eating bere bannocks in Orkney or drinking sahti in Finland. His perspective focused upon every angle of historical record and aesthetic impression. Under his tutelage, French and Belgian *cuisine à la bière* achieved prominence at the first Belgian beer luncheon held in America, hosted at New York's sumptuous Pierre Hotel in Manhattan.

These were royal libations, indeed. Major public figures – the Taoiseachs Seán Lemass, Garrett FitzGerald and Bertie Aherne, Rudy Giuliani, the mayor of New York and HRH The Prince of Wales – found it chic to associate with Jackson. He spurned overindulgence. His esoteric lectures focused on taste, local colour and artisan craftsmanship. He inspired at venues held by the National Geographic Society and Smithsonian Institution in Washington DC, the University of Pennsylvania Museum of Archaeology and Anthropology, Cornell University, the Culinary Institute of America, the Cambridge Union and internationally acclaimed drink and food festivals, including the Speyside Whisky Festival, Great American Beer Festival, Beer Passion Weekend, International Whisky Festival (Netherlands), and Salone del Gusto in Turin, Italy.

The German Academy of Gastronomy was the first to recognise him in 1977, for excellence in beer writing. He was the first recipient of the American-based Brewers Association Recognition Award in 1987, and the Achievement Award from the Institute for Fermentation Studies. He won five Glenfiddich Awards and the Glenfiddich Trophy, as well as the André Simon Award. In 1997, his membership in the Belgian Confederatie der Brouwerijen van België/Confédération des Brasseries de Belgique elevated him as the first non-brewer to receive this honour. He was a Master of the Quaich in Scotch whisky's international trade society, the Keepers of the Quaich, and an Officer of Honour in La Chevalerie du Fourquet des Brasseurs.

His book, *Scotland and its Whiskies*, received the Jury Grand Prize Golden Laurel by the Swiss organization Historica

Gastronomica Helvetica and was selected Best Book on Spirits in the Gourmand World Cookbook Awards 2001. In 2004, he received the Lifetime Achievement Award from *Whisky Magazine*. His book *Whisky: The Definitive World Guide* won five international awards, including the James Beard Award in 2006. After his death, Oxford Brooks University Library at Headington Campus, Oxford, established the Michael Jackson Collection from the priceless contents of his office in London.

Over the course of 30 years, he supported CAMRA in Britain, fuelled the craft beer renaissance in America, ignited the cask ale movement in Japan, and turned new focus on the developing markets of Poland, Italy, and Turkey. Whatever the request, he strove to oblige, whether it be to critique a dram, autograph a book or a breast, or assist a supplicant on the street.

Parkinson's Disease, complicated by diabetes, chipped at his arduous schedule for the better part of ten years. He described himself as 'a man who seeks to sustain his spirit in a battered brain and broken body by invoking Yorkshire stubbornness, the belief that Huddersfield will one day get their hands back on the Rugby League Cup (preferably by wresting it from St Helens), the beliefs of Vince Lombardi, and the Jewish survival instinct.'

To an audience unaware of his afflictions (at a time when he drank the least), he appeared to 'have a drinking problem' – garrulous in speech, rocking like Slam Stewart, off balance, or frozen in mid-step. In December 2006, he disclosed his closely guarded diagnosis to his publishers and adherents, proposing to document his privacy in a painfully honest book entitled *I Am Not Drunk* ...

... but he could still shoot hoops.

On a handful of occasions, Michael would inscribe a few loving words to me in books of his own selection. The last one he added was in an anthology of his work, translated into Italian by Slow Food Editore. It was New Year's Day, 2007. Scribbled onto the first page of *Storie nel bicchiere – di birra, di whisky, di vita*, he wrote,

> ' ... Did John Lennon send you? The next rite of
> passage is toasted in Victory ... '

All too soon, the White Rose of Yorkshire segued into his next rite of passage.

Our lips lay parched, and we thirst for more.

CHAPTER TWO

WHEN'S THE RIGHT TIME
FOR BARLEY WINE?

Stephen Beaumont

There is a restaurant near where I live – 'brasserie,' you'd probably be tempted to call it, given its quite evident Francophilia, although its owners prefer the more generic 'bistro' – which my wife and I frequent with some regularity. We do not go there because the city's restaurant reviewers heap praise upon its cuisine, nor do we offer it our patronage because 'everybody knows (our) name(s),' as the song goes. Seldom do we partake of its massive wine cellar, preferring instead to order by the glass or carafe, and it's certainly not an establishment I would rate alongside the best beer destinations in the city.

No, we eat and drink at Le Select in Toronto because we like the overall *feel* of the place.

Truth be told, if you took the restaurant's cassoulet or ris de veau or croque monsieur and served them to me at another premises, as good as they are, I doubt I would wax rhapsodic in their praise. If you handed to me elsewhere Le Select's drinks menu, I'd likely comment that it was not bad, pretty good, in fact, but nothing to get overly excited about. And while I've never had cause to fault the service at the restaurant, neither is it what you might typify as over-the-top or in some way exceptional.

In other words, it is not one specific part that makes Le Select Bistro attractive to us, but rather the cumulative whole. Service, food, drink or atmosphere alone wouldn't be enough, but taken together they make this fine and welcoming *boîte* one of our favourite places in the city.

What does all this have to do with beer, you ask? Plenty.

Like any fine restaurant, no beer exists as an entity unto itself. We do not imbibe our pints of bitter in a vacuum any more than we sip strong Belgian ales free from the influences of the people, structures and events surrounding us or gulp Pilsner from statuesque sleeves while stuck in some sort of arcane, beer drinker's limbo. For a moment, however brief, our beverage might occasionally define us, but there exists not a single second in which we do not define our drink.

Call it the contextualisation of beer. Its influence is as potent as it is common, to wit, scenario 1: April is disappointed with the quality of the Irish stout she gets in her hometown. As an occasional visitor to Dublin, she is often heard complaining to friends that 'the stout they drink in Ireland is so much better than the stuff we get over here.' Scenario 2: having discovered a spectacular new lager while on vacation in the Caribbean, Henry is convinced it is one of the finest beers he has ever tasted, if not the finest. When he buys a case of it at home, however, he finds that it doesn't hold quite the same appeal.

What April and Henry have discovered, even if they're not quite fully aware of it, is that when you take a beer out of its natural element, it changes ... well ... elementally. April doesn't like the draught stout at her local not because it's that much different from what she drinks in Ireland, but because she's not enjoying her pint in a centuries-old Dublin pub that oozes with atmospheric charm. And Henry is disappointed by his tropical lager at home because he is no longer sunning himself on a white sand beach without a care in the world, idly sipping from an ice-cold bottle. In each of these scenarios, the beer has been idealised, and while each brew may remain the same combination of barley, hops, water and yeast whether at home or away, when stripped of this context, they become quite different beer experiences.

This is the simplest and most obvious example of contextual-isation, and yet the frequency with which it is ignored is staggering. To my experience, almost anyone who has ever vacationed in a sunny clime will have a story of a great beer enjoyed which somehow seemed less great at home. And speak to any stout-sipping patron at an ersatz 'Irish' pub in North America and the odds are high they will rate their pint much lower than that which is supped across the pond. So strong is this latter association, in fact, that it will even be espoused by people who have never set foot in Ireland.

It is both blessing and curse to the people behind the beer, of course. On the one hand, they have a strong association which they can, and do, readily exploit to the betterment of their sales, whether through an evocative and high-profile advertising campaign or something as simple as a poster or piece of local imagery featured at the pub or store. On the other hand, however, once the beer is removed from its favourable context, the consumer is set up for a disappointment that comes as no fault of the brewer, importer or retailer, as witnessed in the hypothetical but all-too-real case studies offered above.

Even so, place and mood are just the tip of the contextual iceberg when it comes to beer. To arrive at the heart of the matter, we will have to dig a little deeper.

Day, Month or Year

Time is another factor in beer taste, be it measured in hours or years. Even the progress of a single day can affect a person's perception of a beer, as I found in an experiment I conducted several years ago for the American whisky and beer magazine, the *Malt Advocate*.

At the time, I was holding my regular tastings of beers and spirits at the Universal Critics Tasting Hour of late morning, usually around 11:00 or so. The theory behind this choice has been well documented and was certainly recognised by me at the time – the palate is at its most sensitive an hour or two before lunch, when the flavours of coffee and breakfast are well behind and the anticipation of the noontime meal is growing. Additionally, for a non-morning person like myself, the late morning also marked the arrival of a significant period of alertness, which would presumably help with detailed flavour perception.

Still, I wondered what my taste buds would be like at other

times of the day and questioned why I was accepting at face value a notion I had not personally put to the test. So, to allay such concerns, I developed an experiment.

To set up my test, I first requested and received from the brewery a six-pack of the freshest Anchor Steam Beer possible, figuring that this brand, which was and remains more-or-less nationally available in the United States, would be instantly recognisable to the majority of the magazine's readers. I then arranged a day during which I would be able to sample a fresh bottle without interruption at six different key periods, beginning with first thing in the morning, then just before lunch, shortly after lunch, late in the afternoon, following dinner, and finally, just prior to bedtime. During each tasting I planned to record detailed notes.

Most of what I found during the day fascinated but did not surprise me. The two tastings that were both most detailed in notes and closest in recorded content were the late morning and late afternoon sessions – precisely the times that common wisdom decreed my senses would be at their most acute. My post-mealtime samplings were the least perceptive – again, in accordance with popular belief – and my late-evening one fell somewhere in the middle. That last bottle, incidentally, was also the most welcome of all the tastings, since it was the first beer of the day I actually allowed myself to finish.

What did come as a bit of a shock was the intensity of my first Anchor Steam, sampled immediately after I awoke and before I indulged in my morning coffee or orange juice. The hoppiness of the beer, which, for those who have not tasted this icon of American craft brewing, is modest by US standards, I perceived as a strong, almost intense bitterness, while the complexity of the malt quotient was virtually lost on me. Reviewing my notes the next day, I concluded that at such an hour, strong flavours taste stronger while subtleties are muted.

The other surprise came from my aroma notes, which remained pretty much identical for each of the six nosings. From this, I deduced that either the more perceptive sense of smell is far less affected by time and circumstance than is taste, or aroma memories are far more acute and persuasive than are those of flavour. To date, I have not yet drawn a conclusion as to which is the correct assumption.

As much as the time of day can play havoc with taste – and here I should stress that there were significant variations in the notes I recorded during my day of tasting – the years can make the effects of a mere 24-hour period seem positively insignificant. Just ask your average beer 'ticker.'

With the popularity of beer rating sites on the Internet has come a new breed of beer reviewer, one who allows little if any room for doubt in the verity of their notes and is consumed by the desire to record on their preferred website as many tastings, or 'ratings,' in their preferred jargon, as they possibly can. In my considerable experience, such individuals often base their evalua- tions on a sip or three of a beer shared among many and, during beer-tasting parties and festivals, continue to make notes long after their palate has been made dumb by alcohol and hops. They are also frequently among the first to authoritatively declare that such-and-such a beer 'is not what it used to be.'[1]

While it is unquestionably true that certain beers have changed and will continue to do so over time, it is equally and perhaps more valid to note the changing palates of those who enjoy them. To someone trying a Sierra Nevada Pale Ale from California for the first time in the early 1980s, for example, it must have seemed a spectacularly hoppy beer, a virtual assault on the taste buds. (I first sampled this now ubiquitous vanguard of the craft brewing movement a few years later, to much the same effect.) For that pioneering soul, Sierra Pale could have been the gateway to a life of craft beer enjoyment or a barrier to further exploration, but it almost certainly made an impact, and a forceful one at that.

Fast forward a quarter century or so, however, and that same beer is at the lower end of bitterness for craft-brewed ales, long since eclipsed by aggressive, domestically brewed pale ales, IPAs and so-called 'double' IPAs, also known as imperial pale ales. What was once a hammer of hoppiness is now, comparatively, a benign brew found across the United States and beyond, in fine-dining restaurants, speciality beer bars and sports lounges alike.

Scroll through some beer chat boards, however, and you will doubtless not scroll long before you come to a post bemoaning how Sierra Pale has changed through the years, becoming more pedestrian in taste and – the ultimate insult these types employ – 'mainstream.' Forget how their context of the beer within the American 'beerscape' has changed, these folks base their opinions on what they are tasting today and believe they tasted in the past.

Problem is, what they think they tasted long ago is not so much what their palates actually experienced as it is their contextualised perception of the beer when first tasted. Sierra Pale was amongst the hoppiest of ales at the time, their argument goes, and it is no longer, thus it must have changed over the years, never mind that the definition of 'hoppy' has changed immeasurably since. And more importantly, never mind how their perception of bitterness has changed over the same period.

Interestingly, and rather curiously, that same ticker who so fully dismisses the role time plays in the contextualisation of taste is often the first to make allowances for the effects of weather, specifically heat, on the flavour of a beer. Yes, I refer here to the famed 'lawnmower beer.'

As anyone who has ever reached for a cold beer as a salve on a scorching and sweaty day will attest, certain beers simply taste better in hot weather than do others. Complete an hour or two of exertion under a high July sun, for example, and it's likely a cold Pilsner will find preference over, say, a sweet stout or barley wine. Hence the common ticker observation that 'it's an okay lawnmower beer.'

Talk about damning with faint praise! But still, at least it does acknowledge that the meteorological context of a brew can sometimes have a strong impact on how its flavour is perceived. Problems arise, however, when what's good for the proverbial goose winds up being utterly unfair to the poor old gander.

Here, the issue is not making allowances for the Pilsner under favourable conditions, but rather, the failure to make concessions for the ill effects that stifling heat may have on a bigger, fuller bodied and alcoholic ale such as the aforementioned barley wine.

Beers such as these, including everything from imperial stouts to doppelbocks, will certainly get tasted in the summer, or sampled in a packed and muggy bar-room, and assessed without concern to how these conditions will negatively affect their enjoyment. No 'lawnmower' beers these, and no quarter given, either, irrespective of the fact they would be best slowly sipped beside a roaring fire in coldest February.

At least these omissions of context are made only on the part of a rarified few. When we all, at least from time to time, neglect to weigh external factors in our beer appreciation, that is when we enjoy a bottle or pint with food.

At the Table

Beer and food pairing is a field that has seen considerable coverage thus far in the 21st century and as much as it is heralded by some as the path to respectability for beer, it is dismissed equally by others as an affectation that reeks of wine-snob pretentiousness. It's a schism that has fostered considerable debate in the brewing world over the years.

Advocates of beer and food partnerships point out that an exceptional pairing can be a delectable thing, taking two separate but wonderful tastes and by joining them, creating a gastronomic experience that is greater than the sum of its individual parts. (Not for nothing are such pairings referred to as beer and food 'marriages.') Detractors, on the other hand, note beer's historic role as the unifier of humankind, enjoyed in pubs and bars by barons of industry and diggers of ditches alike, and suggest that anointing it as accompaniment to specific dishes served atop white tablecloths is to do disservice to this tradition.

I say, why can't it be both? Immediately after which I note that regardless of your position on the matter, the wrong food can and will destroy a beer, just as the wrong beer can and will obliterate the taste of a specific dish.

Interestingly, the most common areas where this kind of gustatory conflict takes place involve the very foods most readily identified with beer, which is to say salty, spicy and oily fare. Think pretzels, chicken wings, cured meats, fish and chips, and deep-fried anything; all of which will annihilate a beer that lacks at least some significant hoppiness.

Where this clash most often takes place is at a Mexican or Indian restaurant, where fiery fare is regularly consumed alongside ice-chilled bottles of the popular national lagers, all conspicuously lacking in hoppiness. There, the cold beer is presented as a salve to the heat of the food, but it's the frigidity that makes it work, not the beer itself. Served cold enough, the light golden lager will anaesthetise the palate, leaving the oily spice on the tongue but freezing the taste buds and, more importantly, the nerves which feel the sting of the food. When the body regulates the temperature of the mouth, the spiciness returns, prompting the diner to reach for another swig of beer, and so on. Great for beer sales, perhaps, but lousy for the enjoyment of a meal.

On the other hand, turn to a hoppy pale ale or IPA with the same fare and the effect is quite different. These beers, served chilled but not frozen, will strip some of the heat from the palate with their cleansing bitterness, leaving the flavour of the spice intact but tempering the pain. Better still, the lingering bitterness of the beer once swallowed will further clean up the taste buds and ready them for the next taste, which will seem like a new experience rather than the piling of hot pepper atop hot pepper.[2]

Salty foods also cause problems for beer, and it is here that the greatest ills are meted out to otherwise deserving brews. Where significant maltiness is present in a beer, salt is the great destroyer. Simply put, salt steals body from the sweet malt of beers like Belgian or Belgian-style abbey ales or German bocks. So a chocolatey Trappist dubbel or caramelly doppelbock, or even a Belgian- or German-style wheat beer, will have its taste drastically altered if it is casually imbibed alongside a basket of chips or bowl of salted mixed nuts, as the salt negatively reacts with the beer's natural sweetness. The lower alcohol beers, the wheats and even some milds, will turn thin and perhaps even a bit papery, while the stronger and bolder brews will, in the worst-case scenario, turn faintly rubbery or even petrol-like in flavour.

Bitter, hoppy beers, on the other hand, will react to salt much the way they do to spice, cleansing the palate and stripping the taste buds so the beer's character remains true, and as an added bonus, the salty foods taste fresh and vibrant with each mouthful.

Similarly, and as much as beer does generally pair well with sweet foods like cakes, mousses and other desserts, sugar can pose a problem for beer. In this case, however, it's a matter of correctly matching like characteristics.

Beer is a marvellous partner with sweets of all sorts. Certainly in comparison with our old friend wine, beer has strengths to spare when it comes to service with the last course of the meal: fruit beers with fruit tarts, strong and spicy Belgian ales with custards and crème brulées, barley wines with Christmas puddings. Indeed, it seems as if there is an ale or lager for every dessert, so long as – and here's the caveat – the sweetness of the beer exceeds that of the dessert.

This is a pivotal point. When the dessert dish, be it cake or custard or pie, possesses a sugar level higher than that of the beer, said ale or lager will almost inevitably suffer in comparison. To get an idea of how this works, think of the effect you get when biting into an apple or orange after having just used peppermint tooth-paste – as fresh and juicy as the fruit may be, its natural sweetness stands not a chance against the intensely perceived sweetness of a mouthful of mint, and so it winds up tasting more sour than sweet.

This same effect will happen when a beer tastes less sweet than the sugar-rich dessert it is meant to accompany. Rather than showing forth its rich maltiness, the beer will lose impact and seem thinner and more austere, even, in cases of extreme difference, sour. When these components are reversed, with the beer being sweeter than the dish, the opposite effect does not happen because the beer is more transient on the palate than will be any dessert, so there's no chance of its sweetness hanging around to lessen the character of the dish.

This effect is mitigated to a large degree when chocolate is involved, principally because the primary ingredient in chocolate, cocoa, possesses a strong component of bitterness. So even when it is sweetened, chocolate possesses a flavour profile which is broadly similar to that of many beers, including stouts and strong porters, barley wines and numerous strong Belgian and Belgian-style ales.

The Look of Beer

Turning finally to less tangible and, it must be admitted, less empirically verifiable areas of contextual tasting, the aesthetics of a beer can have a significant impact upon its assessment. No doubt, that's something with which the majority of Belgian beer aficionados would agree.

Unique among the world's brewers, Belgians are borderline obsessive about the appearance of their beers. For each and every brand produced in the country, there is a glass, and not just a generic, straight-sided vessel embossed with the name of the brand, but a thing of curves, flourishes, accents and sometimes great beauty. Some are of a symbolic nature, such as the chalice-like glasses used in various forms by each of the Trappist monastery breweries, while others have a functional role to fill, as with the aroma-funneling, snifter-shaped goblets meant for strong or spiced ales, but all have an individuality about them as great as the beers they represent.

To gauge the impact of these glasses, you need only watch one being served in a non-Belgian bar or restaurant. Heads turn as tray, bottle and glass is transported through the room, eyes widen as the pouring ritual is observed tableside, and smiles on the faces of observing patrons betray the understanding that this person has just been served *something special.* Quite often, this exercise leads another customer to order the same beer, and you can bet that when they receive their own glass, the beer inside will taste much better than it would were it to be offered in an ordinary chilled tumbler.

Belgians, being very much the aesthetes, appreciate this impact, so much so that certain cafés will refuse to serve a specific beer unless they have the proper glass clean and ready for use. If you order it when all existing glasses have already been served, well, too bad; you will have to wait.

The observations noted thus far represent only a few examples of the contextualisation of flavour in beer. There are others, sufficient to fill a book, as a colleague remarked to me when I noted to him the topic of this essay, but to continue onward would be to gild the lily. The most common and elemental instances have been covered, and the remainder will await further exploration on another day.

In the meantime, it is enough that we all pursue our tasting pleasures with the knowledge and understanding that is not the beer we drink which defines us, as advertising types would like us to think, but rather, we and the circumstances that surround us which define our beer.

NOTES

1 Before I continue in this vein, and to avoid personal assault by roving gangs of sensitive beer tickers, I should quickly add that the type described above is not necessarily the norm among the denizens of the beer-rating sites, several of whom I know and respect, but rather the vocal minority largely responsible for the creation of the ticker stereotype.

2 Those who make the counter-claim that national beers should by definition go with national foods miss an important historic point. For countries whose cuisine has evolved alongside their beers, this is undoubtedly true, witness the UK, Germany and Belgium, amongst others. But Mexico never had an indigenous brewing industry, or at least not one that is sustained today, and neither did India, thus there is no reason that imported beer styles should pair well with their foods. Mezcal and lassi, on the other hand, pair wonderfully with their respective national cuisines.

THREE STEPPS TO ...

Dave Broom

The smell hit you first, the fumey sweetness of whisky-soaked cardboard, a head-thickening, gut-churning blast of alcohol mingling with newly cleaned lino and the stench of early morning evacuations emanating from the row of green-doored cubicles. Hang up the coat and line up to clock in. The panic set in immediately; terrified that I'd have forgotten my number. I was right, I *had* forgotten my number. The queue was building up behind me. 'Get a move on. Fuckinstudent!' came a cry as I scanned the panel containing a hundred identical brown cards. I knew that a failure to clock in on time resulted in you being 'quartered' – a quarter of an hour's wages docked, though I had the distinct feeling that my abuser was thinking of the term's medieval meaning.

A woman off the line asks me my name, grabs the card immediately, shoves it in the machine and pushes me through. 'Best learn it quick son,' she says. Smiles and bustles off. So this was work. The 'fuckinstudents' (as we were doomed to be known) were gathered together in order for the day's tasks to be doled out by one of the brown coats, a lugubrious balding man with glasses.

'You and you, fibre ... you two, dispatch ... you lot ... ' he gestures to the rest of us ... 'you're on the lines ... apart from you son. Get yersel up to the filters.'

Those of us on our second or third year doing this move off to the designated areas. I stand with another newcomer at the end of a line with the brown coat as he takes us through the basics.

'Get a pallet, put the cases on it, then band it. Then start the next. OK?' He moves off. How hard could that be? Picking up boxes?

The line was running, it sounded like a hundred runaway milk floats were heading in my direction. Bottles clashing, clinking, being filled, checked for flies, labelled, capped, boxed. I watched the first case come towards me, the sticky tape pulling the flaps down, the stencil marking the side and then rattling down the rollers.

Heavier than I expect, it slips in my grip and drops on to the front edge of the pallet.

'Wrong way!' shouts Alex from the other line. 'Stick it at the back.' I do.

'Wrong way ... other way roon!' I turn it and go back for the next one. The line is already backed up. Clear them quickly and slowly begin to build the levels.

'Five high!'

'Wrong way!'

'Ye reverse the order each layer!'

'Fuck it. Start again.'

He comes over, breaks down the build and shows me. Goes back to his line. I'm sure I hear a muttered, 'Fuckinstudent.'

The shiny surface slips in the fingers, gliding over the image of the two dogs as I humph the next one up to shoulder height, push it above my head and shove it to the back edge.

'Naw naw naw!! Top layer is upside doon!' Now he tells me. Bastard.

'Right. Band it.'

He hands me a strip of plastic tape, passes one edge round the cases, pushes it through a machine, tightens the ends, clips it, cuts it. It seems easy. A forklift is waiting to crash into the pallet and carries it off to despatch. Next pallet is grabbed and off it goes again. It's 8.30am and I'm knackered.

Days like these would start at 6am in the steely light of a Glasgow summer. Dress, mug of tea and walk to the bus stop. Whose idea was it to get a job? A job that started at this time in the morning at that? Fact was I needed one. Money mainly. Out of school, unsure of exam results, needing to get out of a house that was still draped in the memories of my father's recent death. Get over it, get on with it, life goes on and all of that crap. My mother still cried every day and I had no words left. Somehow his death had changed people's view of me, altered my status. The older generation: family friends, relatives, neighbours all said how 'mature' I had suddenly become. My uncle, a remote though kindly man, had begun to take me to pubs and buy me whisky.

I was just 18, but there were shoes to fill, shoes that were still lined up in the wardrobe under empty suits which I'd never grow into. Maybe unconsciously this investing of notional maturity was the easiest way in which they could cope with me. Tell him he's an adult and he'll have to grieve like one. Which meant being stoically Scottish and getting a job. Nothing like the Protestant work ethic for driving emotion out of the equation. So I did.

My uncle, who worked for WP Lowrie, the sherry and wine arm of James Buchanan (aka Black & White) told me they were needing temporary labour at the Stepps bottling plant to help with the ramping up of production that took place before the plant closed for the Galsgow Fair holiday fortnight. I filled in the form. Got the job. So what if it was on the other side of the city?

A strange, silent, crew on these early morning buses. Shift workers, cleaners, functionaries, the invisible transportation of the working class. Folk from the Drum, Knightswood, Temple, Anniesland. Empty streets festooned with last night's litter, graffiti on window shutters, locked pubs, newsagents, black-eyed windows. A boat adrift in the showroom of Clyde Chandlers, beached among sandstone reefs and porcelain wally closes.

Maybe my hollowness suited the early mornings. My fellow passengers too were just shells heading into town to be filled up by whatever mundane task they needed to do in order to live.

I had to change at Buchanan Street bus station from the tricolour-clad Glasgow Corporation bus to the blue fleet which serviced the outer suburbs; you can always rely on Glasgow's inability to keep its sectarianism under wraps. Past Dennistoun, Riddrie, my dad's birthplace, the Bar-L out to Stepps on the fringes, not quite Glasgow, not quite the planned paradise of Cumbernauld.

It was a newish plant, considered high-tech for the time, semi-automated, dedicated to bottling Black & White, but also Gordon's gin, Ballantine's (for some reason) and small runs of unknown blends. After a couple of weeks I was into the swing of things. Learned the hierarchy. Fuckinstudents were at the bottom of the pile, then there were shop-floor workers, shop stewards, brown coats, white coats and then suits. There was clear demarcation between all the groups and you stuck to your own clique. By now, I'd learned the new geometry of each of the 'builds,' even mastered the '96 build' I had struggled with on the first day. The secret was to start at the back corner and build it up in a wedge shape from there, but never completing the base layer until the last moment. There was strange beauty to see it coming together, knowing the right tension on the banding, pulling until the tape began to bite through the outer surfaces.

We all prayed for the Black & White lines as they had the easiest builds. If you were lucky you might get the speciality line, slow-moving and dedicated to the big sizes and miniatures. Heavy as fuck the boxes were, but they only came down to you once every five minutes or so. No-one wanted the gin line. For some reason gin seemed to be easier to bottle than whisky so the pace was frantic; as the cases were only stacked three high it was head down and get tore in, standing in a permanent crouch flinging them on to the pallet for 40 minutes.

Three guys would work two lines. Twenty minutes on one, 20 minutes on the other, then a 20-minute break.

'It's your spell son.'

I was always son ... or fuckinstudent. As you weren't allowed to leave the shop floor, the only place to sit was the gents' toilet. As it wasn't an official break there was no chance of a cup of tea, unlike the mugs of the brown coats sitting in their elevated office.

The bog it was then. A cream door, tiled, two cubicles, a urinal and men, standing, leaning, sitting, smoking, shitting, having a piss, talking horses and football, reading the paper. A nod from one of them.

'Ye'll huv a drink.' The words were an order rather than a polite suggestion.

'Aye. Sure ... thanks.'

I cast around for what he was talking about. Then a hand went into the cistern and hauled out a bottle, hot off the line. Drams would be passed around. That was breakfast dealt with then. I wondered whether to pull the Kerouac out of my pocket. Thought better of it. There was time for that on the bus.

The day stopped being about work and became more of a long drinking session interrupted by bouts of activity. Whisky breath was a sign of camaraderie, membership of a gentlemens' club. Inevitably, productivity dropped significantly in the afternoons; cases would be dropped, bands wouldn't be tightened fully and the forklift drivers, equally hammered, would cowp entire pallets. The floor was awash with drink. No-one really seemed to mind as another seeping carton was heaved into the waste. If you didn't love whisky by the end of this, you were in the wrong job.

'You ... fibre!'

I'm being led upstairs to where the empty cases are kept. Never quite worked out why it was called 'fibre.' Packing would be more accurate. A dim, dusty place occupied solely by men too old for the speedy manual labour of the lines. A silent cardboard city, skyscrapers of made-up boxes, suburbs of flatpacks, blocks of liners, decorated with monochrome labels: the two dogs, House of Commons, Royal Household.

'In here son.'

I was led through a maze of cardboard to hidden bothies in the middle where there were boxes for chairs, a case for a table and in a niche excavated in the brown walls, a secret compartment holding the inevitable bottle and packs of cards.

'Ye'll huv a drink.'

You could hear the brown coats coming round, calling out. One of the men would leave by another passage, find out what job had to be done and return. In reality there was little work. I felt older by the second, as if the cardboard was seeping into my veins. Looking at their kind, tired eyes. Maybe they lived there. Never clocked them at the start of the day. Is this how it ends? Forgotten in a hidden bothy? I missed the lines. The noise, the chaos, the smell, the sound of a pallet sclaffing on the floor, the rattle and clink of glass.

I enjoyed the routine, the weird artificiality of the day, the anonymity of being just a fuckinstudent, being free of questions. The simplicity of this life suited my state of mind, the fuzziness of drink, the keys to a new world. It was the summer of '77, a time of change and choices, but big life-changing things like Uni or a job, punk or psychedelia, could be shelved thanks to the blankness of this routine. Just lift your boxes and stott from the end of the line to the bog.

As the Fair drew closer, so the talk was of Benidorm and Alicante. The drinking also seemed to increase. Once, two of us were sharing the Gordon's lines with a full-timer called Billy who had been showing the effects since the early morning. After lunch he didn't return from his spell. We worked on, expecting him to stagger out. Then the word came round that he'd passed out in the bog. We worked on. A brown coat appeared.

'You not on your spell?'

'Just been.'

'You sure?'

'Aye.'

Behind the brown coat's back I could see Billy being stretchered out on a flattened piece of cardboard by his mates. The two of us ran the lines all afternoon. Collapsed at the end of it, but appeared to also have passed a test. We students were tolerated, but we were never part of the workforce. The fact we paid no tax was resented, especially at the end of the week when the fat little envelope of notes was handed out.

'Work less than we do and they get mair money ... fuckinstudents.'

On Fair Friday, after a morning of drinking I was summoned into a room where a white coat dispensed my first (and last) official dram. 'Thank you David,' he said, handing me a glass and my wage packet. I knock it back, quite the drinker now, and head back to the bog where a fellow student has sparked up a joint. It was that kind of place.

The plant is packing up at lunchtime and I stagger to the bus trying not to spin out as the two drugs compete for supremacy. Make it to the bus station and change onto an 11. By the time we've reached Woodlands Road I'm fighting growing nausea. The bus stops. I rush out and run up a close. Vomit. Wipe the mouth and head into Lost Chord to browse the second-hand records.

The lines shut down during the Fair, so we were all sent outside. Some lucky bastards got painting, which seemed to consist of playing football with the paint pots as goalposts. The rest of us were at the Despatch under the tutelage of Big John, a filthy-tempered man prone to cursing and full of wild tales of reckless debauchery.

'Where ye frae son?'

'Kelvindale … you know … west end'

'Posh bastard.'

'Not really … ' I start the explanation that it's not Kelvinside but he's not listening.

'Ye been tae the brothel in Park Street? Fuckin' brilliant place … ' and he launches into a lurid tale involving golden showers.

'Can't say I have John,' says I, dreading that he's going to invite me on his next visit.

It was Big John who taught me how to pack a shipping container. Either by pallet truck, which was tricky enough in its own way, involving nasty little turns, but infinitely preferable to building by hand. Hundreds of cases rammed in from floor to ceiling. Containers may look perfectly rectangular, but they're always out of whack.

'Right you. Get it right in the fuckin' corner. Slam it in!'

I do.

'Now build it.'

It's going fine until the third row when, as the container is out of true, the cases won't fit.

'What you stopped fur?'

'It won't go John.'

'Kick the fucker then.' I poke at the box with my toe.

'Naw. Batter it! Gie it laldy son!'

He demonstrates. I hear the crack of breaking glass, the stain of whisky blooms across the white dog.

'Does it go noo?'

'Aye.'

'Right ye are.'

'But ... '

'Listen son,' he says, 'all of this is bound for ... ' he looks at the case, ' ... Venezuela. You really think thcy Venezuelese'll be bothered by a few fuckin' bottles broken in transit?'

Another lesson learned. From then on we chucked them in. Kicking, stamping, hurling them against the sides to get a true fit, bathing in the fumes.

What I wasn't doing was writing, though that had been the idea. To go to the hills, get away from the city. Instead at the end of the shift I'd get the bus back to Buchanan Street and walk straight to the pub. Dram and a Fowler's Wee Heavy. I had begun to spend more time around Glasgow Cross, the Scotia, the Viccy bar, the licensed bunkers with breeze-blocks for windows and tables screwed to the floor. Pints and wee fat glasses with a quarter gill in them. Old Glasgow. My dad's workplace. Trying to find him, propping up the bar after work. Chewing the fat.

Was this the maturity that they were all talking about? If I was as mature as they said I was, then I was independent and pubs, concert halls and friends' floors were my new homes. This wasn't so much rebellion as rejection of what had (or hadn't happened) before, of social niceties, of silent Sundays, of church. The area where I was brought up was, like many outlying parts of Glasgow, dry. Though there was a nice wee primary school and a row of shops, it was a desperate place for a teenager. If I wanted a new life, wanted to create, then I had to find it in the city, wander the streets. That summer I became Glaswegian, then turned my back on the city and never returned.

The exam results weren't great, but were good enough to get me out of Glasgow a dizzying 30 miles north to Stirling. I'd go back to Stepps the next summer before other jobs filled the summer break: raspberry packing, a clothing warehouse, then life took over. The next time I heard of Stepps was when it was closed down after a huge duty-free scam was uncovered.

It would be too glib to say this is where 'my whisky life' started. This was a job I chanced upon. Neither did it show me a career path, or inculcate a deep love of the complexities of malt and grain. There was no epiphany, no Damascene moment as scales fell from my eyes and I could see clearly. Let's face it, I could barely focus most of the time.

Yet, something happened that summer, maybe in the loo, maybe in the endless wanderings round Glasgow, maybe in the pubs shrouded by cigarette smoke, drinking stale beer and haufs. What that Stepps' summer taught me was about community and how, though I could observe it at work, I could never be part of it; that if I wanted to walk and look and write, then being outside it all, being sat in the corner at a scuffed table with a half-full glass was the way it would have to be. This strange recalibration of self, this state of no-mind acted as some sort of seal.

The healing would come later.

CHAPTER FOUR

PANTS TO WHISKY: AN AUTHENTIC LINK

Ian Buxton

I buy my pants from Marks & Spencer. Lots of people do. But, on a recent visit, I was intrigued to note that the packaging bore the legend 'authentic' and in case of any doubt the pants themselves were embroidered round the waistband with the word itself. Ten times in all, in block capitals: AUTHENTIC. Like that.

This got me to thinking: what exactly is 'authentic' about gents' underwear? And what would a inauthentic pair of pants be like? And then my mind ranged to a deeper topic: what exactly does 'authentic' mean anyway? Does it, in fact, mean anything, or has it been so devalued as to become an entirely empty, if comforting, cliché?

And what does this mean for the marketers of Scotch whisky who, at almost every turn, are anxious to assure us of their authenticity?

Authenticity. Tradition. Heritage. Provenance.

I've come to feel that these represent, as Sherlock Holmes might have observed, quite a three-pipe problem. Knowing nothing of either your reading speed or your patience I am not sure whether more or less than 50 minutes will be required, but bear with me. In fact, get a bottle and glass. This may prove to be a three-dram problem.

Michael Jackson was fond of asking questions. In fact, he never stopped. So, in that spirit and wearing my comfortable new authentic pants, I want to question some of the terms frequently used in the promotion of single malt whisky (and other distilled spirits, as well).

We hear a great deal about 'authenticity' and 'tradition' and their close relatives 'heritage' and 'provenance.' On the face of it they don't seem difficult terms. After all, we all know what they mean, don't we? But scratch the surface and their meaning becomes more opaque.

What, for example, do we mean by 'authenticity' and 'tradition' in the context of distilling practice? These are certainly claims that the distillers themselves are happy to make. A very quick search on the Internet reveals a number of instances. For example:

> 'What a combination: traditional distilling and
> state-of-the-art bottling.' [Bruichladdich][1]
> ' ... the traditions of distilling are as important today
> as they ever were at Morrison Bowmore ... '
> [Morrison Bowmore][2]

These or similar quotations could be repeated *ad nauseum* from almost any distiller's website, corporate brochure or brand advertising, especially for single malts. But what do they mean? I submit that we can legitimately question how 'traditional' most Scotch whisky distilling is today without demeaning either the product, or the distillers. Moreover, strict adherence to a 'tradition' (however 'authentic' that version of history may be) may hold dangers to Scotch whisky's long-term global future.

But where do we start? How 'traditional' do we have to be to be 'authentic'? Take Bruichladdich for example. The company describe the production process in the following terms:

> ' ... an unusual marriage of manual 19th-century
> equipment, inspirational distillery design and
> pre-industrial distilling techniques.'[3]

Bruichladdich was built in 1881 and when Alfred Barnard visited a few years later, he noted that the two stills were 'both heated by fire' and that the annual output was 94,000 gallons (426,760 litres).[4] Today, Bruichladdich has four stills and, in common with most of the rest of the industry, all are indirectly fired.

After some expansion around 1960, two additional stills were installed as recently as 1975 and increased the distillery's capacity to 800,000 proof gallons, or around eight-and-a-half times that observed by Barnard.

The company's own very informative history on the Bruichladdich website also informs us that barley was hoisted to the barley loft by horse until the late 1950s, when it was mechanised. So it's clear from this reference that Bruichladdich maintained the maltings seen by Alfred Barnard until that date at least. It is not, in fact, immediately clear when malting ceased. However, though Bruichladdich retain an ambition to reopen their maltings, at the time of writing all the malt is sourced externally.

Looking more widely, historians broadly agree that the Industrial Revolution began in England sometime after 1760 and the so-called Second Industrial Revolution around 1850 when technological and economic progress gained momentum with the successful application of steam power to ships and railways or, as at Bruichladdich, the 'powerful steam engine' mentioned by Barnard.[5]

Certainly, by 1881, the Industrial Revolution was fully established and our Victorian forbears were proud of this fact, as witness the Great Exhibition of 1855 and the subsequent hugely popular series of similar events. It's only a guess, but I rather think that Bruichladdich's founder William Harvey would be somewhat offended to have his creation described as 'pre-industrial.' In fact, elsewhere on the company's website the 1881 distillery is described as 'state of the art' for its period, which seems both kinder and more accurate.[6]

So let's see: Bruichladdich is both 'pre-industrial' and 'state of the art' for 1881, well into the Industrial Revolution; the distillery is still 'traditional' despite having abandoned on-site malting and direct-fired stills and having been substantially expanded in 1975;

it uses 'manual 19th-century equipment' but dropped the man and his horse in the 1950s in favour of a mechanical hoist. I can imagine that they were both grateful.

So when did this 'authenticity' and 'tradition' start? In 1975, when the distillery was expanded? In the 1950s when Dobbin was retired? When direct firing was abandoned? In 1881? In fact, Bruichladdich appear to select quite arbitrarily from their history to support their own marketing myths – and, it's only fair to observe, so do the majority of their competitors. History, it seems, is a bran tub from which we can selectively pluck shiny new apples.

I could go on, or I could have taken another distillery as an example almost at random, because my purpose here is not to pick on Bruichladdich. In fact, most commentators would consider Bruichladdich 'traditional' in its operation, and thus 'authentic,' without perhaps fully considering the meaning of this emotionally charged vocabulary. I will add also in my defence that I respect their whisky greatly; enjoy it and even bought a cask of new fillings when the distillery re-opened as a practical demon-stration of my support and enthusiasm for the project.

So, I repeat, these observations are not about Bruichladdich's products, but about the language used to market them and what we mean and what we think we mean by that. It's actually quite a serious philosophical problem. American 'experience' gurus Joe Pine and Jim Gilmore define it as 'the authenticity paradox,' going on to comment:

> ' ... all human enterprise in *ontologically* unreal – that is,
> in its very being, it is inauthentic; and yet, much output
> from that enterprise is *phenomenologically* real – that is,
> perceived as authentic by the individuals who buy
> them.'[7]

This isn't all just semantics and academic carping, by the way. What we mean by 'authentic' and 'traditional' actually matters and is of considerable commercial importance. We shall return to the question of perceived authenticity later. To consider the issue of commercial significance, we have to turn to the distillery itself.

Traditional Practice

Consider the changes there have been to traditional distilling practice in the last hundred years. For an apparently conservative, traditional and unchanging industry, they have, in fact, been radical. Let's list some of the most important. Varieties of barley have changed greatly; leaving aside primitive and long-abandoned strains such as bere, in the last 50 years there has been much innovation. Golden Promise accounted for close to 95% of the Scottish barley crop in the 1960s but declined to 13% by 1987 and has since fallen further out of favour. It was overtaken by Triumph, Optic and Chariot. More recently, varieties such as Quench, Publican and Tartan are being trialled.

The aim here is to develop strains that are hardy, disease-resistant and give the highest yields. That, of course, leads to the question of malting. In fact, like Bruichladdich, many distillers had abandoned their own maltings by the 1970s and large specialist firms now dominate the malting business. Techniques here have changed: floor maltings make up a tiny percentage of the output, being retained as much for their marketing value and tourist appeal as any other factor and most malt comes from giant, industrialised complexes.

It is no longer possible to write, as Aeneas MacDonald did in 1930, that, 'The convenient proximity of a peat bog is an economic necessity for a Highland malt distillery'[8] as the use of peat to dry malted barley is largely confined to Islay, Orkney and a few Speyside expressions largely targeted at single malt enthusiasts. The peaty taste of mainstream whisky, especially in blends, is for the most part a thing of the past.

Once inside the distillery we can observe further changes: influenced by the brewing industry, mash tuns have grown in size and at least one mash filter has been quietly introduced; open hot-wort aerators and wort refrigerators are a thing of the past;[9] yeast strains have changed; fermentation is more carefully controlled; still technology has evolved (even if still shapes and sizes appear to have become fixed to individual distillery patterns), direct-firing and the use of the rummager have disappeared at the behest of health and safety legislation and increased energy efficiency; the temperatures of the stills are now controlled precisely by computer so the addition of soap is no longer needed as an anti-foaming surfactant; worm tubs have largely been replaced by shell and tube condensers; wood management (not to mention the introduction of 'finishing') is unrecognisable from 50 years ago and traditional dunnage warehouses have given way to enormous computer-controlled buildings, with racks of anonymous casks identified only by a sterile barcode.

Substances such as paxarette (a very sweet, dark sherry-based substance) have followed its dubious predecessors such as 'Hamburg sherry,' 'prune wine' and 'cocked hat spirit' into the dark cellars of whisky's history and are no longer mentioned in polite company, though if one was feeling mischievous they might be considered traditional practices.

However, paxarette was still common enough in recent years for Philp[10] to write in 1989 that ' ... a typical current cooperage procedure in the Scotch Whisky industry is to add 500ml of Paxarette per hogshead, or 1 litre per butt, pressurise at 48 kPa (7psig) for 10 min and then disgorge any unabsorbed Paxarette.'

In fairness, however, he also goes on to observe that ' ... the true "sherry shipping cask" flavour ... has never been reproduced by this treatment.'

At one time, direct firing was considered an essential ingredient in the flavour of single malt whisky. Sir Walter Gilbey, proprietor of Glenspey, Strathmill and Knockando distilleries, wrote an impassioned defence of direct firing in 1904.[11]

It is a curious fact that the heat of the fire also imparts a Flavour to the vapourised matter. The fire heat gives the spirit a character which distinguishes it from Spirits distilled by the Patent Still. It imparts to the Spirit the character known as empyreumatic[12], which is easily recognised in the product of the Pot Still and which is quite absent in Spirit produced by the Patent Still.

Such a view was still current in the 1950s. SH Hastie[13] wrote:

During this process of boiling of the wash over a naked fire, changes take place in the constituents of the wash prior to and during distillation which are vital to the flavour and character of the whisky. Flavour and character do not *originate* in the Still as they are dependent on other factors – principally the local water supply – but, if the wash were distilled in a still which was heated, say, by steam, the same intensity of character and quality would not be obtained.

Today, direct firing is all but a memory (Glenfiddich is a notable exception) and the rummager, traditional or not, confined to the museum. Where once distilling was a labour-intensive process and even the smallest distillery employed a dozen or more men, today even the largest plants, such as Chivas Brothers' re-modelled Glenburgie, can be managed by one operator seated at a computer console.

It's hard to deny that the cumulative effect of all this has been to alter the taste of whisky (which, of course, was originally drunk without the benefit of ageing). Whilst the fundamental chemical processes going on in a distillery are unchanged from when distilling was first invented, today's distillery would be all but unrecognisable to a George Smith or an Alfred Barnard.

So how far is today's distillery and the whisky it produces 'traditional'?

New Regulations

'So what?' you may well enquire. Well, to illustrate the commercial significance of all this consider the new EU regulations on the description of whisky, promoted by the Scotch Whisky Association (SWA) and DEFRA (the UK Government's Department for Environment Food & Rural Affairs).

Much ink was spilled on the vexed question of the 'blended malt' category and passions ran high. But, tucked away in the small print of the document was another, equally contentious new definition that passed almost unnoticed. On page 4 of the consultation document,[14] various types of whisky were defined, single malt being described in the following terms:

'Single Malt Scotch Whisky' means a Scotch Whisky
that has been distilled –
(a) at a single distillery;
(b) from water and malted barley without the addition
of any other cereals; and
(c) by batch distillation in pot stills.

Nothing new or controversial there you would imagine. In fact, clause c) which requires single malt to be distilled in batches in a pot still was new. Again, 'so what?' you may be asking. This innocuous-looking clause was the source of much hand-wringing at Loch Lomond Distillers of Alexandria, near Glasgow, for there they had been making what they believed to be single malt whisky in a column still. They took a wash made entirely of malted barley and, in a single distillery, ran it through a column still entirely made of copper. Surely this was malt whisky?

They had several good arguments in their favour, notably the process efficiency both in terms of the utilisation of raw materials and energy. Energy and materials efficiency: two aims which spoke directly to industry and government's green concerns and thus an innovation that presumably would be welcomed with open arms?

Moreover, if Loch Lomond could produce acceptable single malt at a significantly reduced cost compared to a pot-still distillery then clearly this was a way of protecting Scotch whisky production from the inevitable competition from lower-cost producers such as China and India? After all, it cannot be very long before entrepreneurs in these burgeoning markets decide that domestic production of 'single malt whisky' can compete aggressively with Scotch.

Loch Lomond weren't even asking to be included in the 'single malt' category but rather argued for a distinct category, making clear the use of a column still. What could be simpler?

Surely this was a legitimate single malt whisky?

'No,' said the SWA. According to their spokesman, quoted in *Scotland on Sunday* newspaper:[15]

> Campbell Evans, Director of Government Affairs at the SWA, said: 'The further category being floated does not reflect traditional Scotch Whisky distillation and practice'.

But are they right? What was 'traditional' practice? (And when does 'traditional' begin and end?)

There's a good case to be made that Loch Lomond could have defended their column still as 'traditional Scotch Whisky distillation.' Historical records show that so-called 'Silent Malt' was widely made in the 19th century. Cameronbridge, Yoker and Glenmavis distilleries all produced such a spirit and there's evidence that the practice also existed elsewhere. Given this, it is therefore as much part of traditional Scotch whisky production as distilling grain whisky in a continuous still. After all, that started out in pot stills and only evolved to the continuous still after 1830. Fighting the arrival of grain and the innovation of blending didn't do the Irish whiskey industry much good (there might just be a lesson from history here).

The practice didn't die out at the end of the 19th century. Probably the most important writer of all time on distilling practice, JA Nettleton notes that the production of 'Patent-still all-malt whisky, as made at one or two distilleries, may claim the title "whisky" with the qualifying description.'[16] In other words, the production of malt whisky in a column still was considered unremarkable in 1913 by the greatest authority of the age.

George Christie produced malt whisky from a continuous still at his North of Scotland Distillery until the 1960s and, obviously, Loch Lomond continues to do so. What is more, both Irish Distillers and Nikka are currently making whiskies of this style. They may not be Scotch whiskies, but clearly this isn't just a one-off and it isn't going to go away.

Continuous-still malt may be unusual, but some would argue

that it has greater historical precedence than the cask finishing which has been adopted by the industry with such glee. If the proposed new rules allow a Lomond still or a modified pot still to make single malt whisky (and they do), then where do we stop? And, by the by, the Lomond still now enshrined in law as 'traditional', was only invented in 1955 by Alistair Cunningham and Arthur Warren for Hiram Walker's Dumbarton plant and installed on an experimental basis at their Inverleven Distillery. Tradition, it seems, exists well within the lifetime of this author!

Not good although drinkable

This may all seem a rather arcane trade dispute. After all, the owners of Loch Lomond Distillery are not members of the SWA who, like any trade association, act primarily to defend the interests of their members, and it may seem to be of little significance to the drinker. Not so.

Consider British manufacturing industry, if you can recall such a thing. Once upon a time, the UK was the manufacturing powerhouse of the world, supplying capital goods to every country round the globe. In living memory it's possible to recall a vibrant British manufacturing industry in cars, televisions and all kind of consumer goods.

Now it's largely gone, undone by the toxic combination of global competition, under-investment, poor management and intransigent trade unionism. A key factor was a lack of innovation: Japanese motor cars and motor cycles undermined a once-thriving UK industry by providing better, more innovative products that fulfilled the needs of an international market.

Could the same thing happen to Scotch whisky? Right now, it seems improbable. The industry is in great health, with record levels of investment, production at an all-time high and exports booming. Moreover, as volumes have increased, prices have increased even faster, leading some to suggest that this is a 'golden age' for Scotch whisky.

But Scotch hasn't always been the leader of the pack. In the late 19th century the four great Dublin firms of John Jameson, William Jameson, John Power and George Roe dominated the global market. Irish pot-still whiskey was the preferred drink and Dublin whiskey considered the finest in the world. Hard though it may be to believe, Scotch whisky was shipped to Ireland and immediately re-exported simply to get an Irish Customs' certificate and be sold by unscrupulous merchants as 'Irish whiskey.' Such was the premium commanded by the genuine Dublin product that the cost of shipping was more than made up by the additional price that could be charged for the counterfeit spirit.

In 1878 the Thomas Street, Dublin distillery of George Roe & Co was the largest pot-still distillery in the United Kingdom (and thus the world). Today, like Ozymandias' legs of stone, the only vestige that remains is the curious windmill tower.

There were many reasons for the decline of the Irish industry but the seeds of its destruction lay in the refusal of the leading Dublin distillers to accept the practice of blending. They set their face against that particular innovation, trusting instead to 'traditional practice.' Events were to prove this particular strategy commercially disastrous.

It may be argued, however, that this example is more than 100 years old. But consider: 'Those who forget history are condemned to repeat it.' If George Santayana is right, it is not necessary to step out of living memory to find pertinent lessons, closer to home.

Cast your mind back a little over 50 years. Complacency then characterised the Scotch whisky industry. In an official SWA publication[17], one SH Hastie recorded:

> It is a fact, however, that Scotch Whisky cannot be
> made anywhere else. The Japs came to this country
> years ago, copied our plant, and even employed
> some of our Speyside personnel. They produced an
> imitation of Speyside Whisky which was not good
> although drinkable.

How Hastie must now be turning in his grave! In 2008, Japanese whiskies were voted 'World's Best Blended Whisky' (Suntory Hibiki 30 Years Old) and 'World's Best Single Malt Whisky' (Yoichi 20 Years Old). This was no fluke: in 2007 the 'World's Best Blended Malt Whisky' was also Japanese, as was the 'Best Blended Whisky.'

And this wasn't the aberrant view of just one enthusiast. On the contrary, the 'World's Best' awards are organised by *Whisky Magazine* and involve three rounds of blind tasting, with a rotating panel of expert judges. Having served on the panel, I can testify to the rigour of the procedure and the care and attention given by the judges to their decisions. Only long after the score cards have been collected do we learn the identity of the whiskies.

So if Japanese whisky is now, by one measure at least, leading the world could Scotch whisky go the same way as shipbuilding, Rudge-Whitworth and BSA motorbikes, Standard and Alvis cars and Irish pot-still whiskey? Don't forget, BSA was once the largest manufacturer of motorcycles in the world and, at their peak, less than one hundred years ago, British yards accounted for around 60% of the world's shipping tonnage. There is no intrinsic reason why Scotch whisky is destined for inevitable and continuing success – as the poignant symbol of George Roe & Co's forlorn windmill tower testifies.

Elijah sent his servant seven times to the top of Mount Carmel and in the words of the King James Bible, 'it came to pass at the seventh time, that he said, "Behold, there ariseth a little cloud out of the sea, like a man's hand."'.[18] After that, it rained rather heavily.

I say no more, other than to note that Suntory Europe recently reported that sales of Yamazaki single malt in Europe grew 2,300% (yes, 23 times) between 2003 and 2007. It may have been from a tiny base – a cloud no bigger than a man's hand, in fact, but is there a servant on whisky's Mount Carmel?

Perhaps all this seems ludicrous and alarmist. But perhaps it's worth considering that well within the lifetime of the typical reader of this essay the idea that Jaguar and Land Rover, jewels in the crown of what remains of the British car industry, would be in Indian ownership would have seemed equally absurd.

Plastic cups, anyone?

And that brings us to the question of the Indian whisky market and packaging innovation. Indian 'whisky' is not accepted as such in the European Union as the base spirit is distilled from molasses (it would therefore be classified as rum). Notwithstanding the rights and wrongs of this (and the matter is strenuously debated at governmental level) the Indian domestic consumer drinks around 87 million cases of Indian whisky which is comparable to global sales of slightly less than 86 million cases of Scotch whisky.

Brands such as Bagpiper and McDowells are ubiquitous in India. The names may seem familiar but their PET pre-formed bottles; tamper-evident packaging and single-serve preformed plastic cups (mirroring the pre-packed cups of orange juice on the in-flight breakfast tray) are far removed from the way Scotch whisky is packaged and presented in Western markets. A lot of this Indian packaging innovation looks incongruous to our eyes and much of it fails even in its home market – but they keep trying.

It's generally assumed that there's little we can learn from this. Yet it may just be worth asking: can the lessons from a single market larger than Scotch whisky's global sales be totally ignored? After all, we may reject Indian whisky as being nothing more than rum under another name but an awful lot of consumers appear more than happy with it and are prepared to drink very large amounts of it from a wide variety of packages.

Is Scotch being just the tiniest bit purist here? After all, if we want to conquer the Indian market (and a great deal of the new production capacity currently being constructed in Scotland is based on the firm belief that we do and we can) then isn't it a case of 'when in Rome?'

This seems to me to be at the heart of the problem with the current fixation on authenticity and traditional practice. For perfectly understandable reasons, much of the marketing of Scotch whisky (especially single malt) is based on a more or less explicit claim to authenticity and tradition.

Yet much of this can be questioned and it's undeniable that the twin pressures of efficiency and cost reduction will continue to drive technical innovation within the distillery itself. As a result, distilling practice will inevitably become progressively more and more detached from the image which is potrayed to sell it.

At the same time, the industry as a whole is imposing new restrictions on itself in the name of consumer protection. Is there any compelling evidence that consumers, especially the emergent, newly affluent middle classes of the BRIC nations, actually care? Is Scotch in danger of following Irish whiskey into self-imposed exile? Are the new regulations little more than a self-imposed straightjacket that leaves Scotch like a prehistoric insect preserved in amber? The questions may seem facile but the precedents are there.

Just suppose an Indian or Chinese distiller could offer – at a substantial cost advantage (or at significantly greater profit) – an Indian or Chinese single malt whisky to their domestic market. There is no barrier to such a producer using Loch Lomond's column still technology and quasi-Scotch brands (Bagpiper, McDowells) dominate the Indian market, so why wouldn't they? Where would the fond hopes of new sales for Scotch then stand?

Or what if the Japanese, producers of the 'World's Best' whisky today, decided to embrace this approach? Remember, we're speaking of a mass market here, not the relatively small number of single malt aficionados who will argue long into the night about peating levels and wood finishes. If it looks good, smells good, tastes good and costs less, why would new consumers in the emerging markets not embrace this 'single malt,' irrespective of a highly selective view of traditional practice that arguably owes more to the marketer's art than observed reality?

In ossifying an officially endorsed view of tradition, are the custodians of Scotch whisky not unwittingly emulating those medieval theologians who debated at length 'Whether a Million of Angels may not fit upon a needle's point?'[19]

Remember also that the single malts we all love are dependent on the continued success of big global brands. The sales of

Johnnie Walker, Chivas Regal, Ballantine's, Dewar's and the rest ensure the survival of the single malt distilleries that are essential to their special taste and flavour.

So perhaps – just perhaps – Scotch whisky wants to think long and hard about its future and where its best interests lie. Binding our own hands may not be such a very shrewd move in the long term.

One final lesson from history, and two final questions: in 1878 the Dublin distillers, then leaders of the world market and determined to defend the reputation of pot-still whiskey, set out energetically, and convinced of the justice of their cause, 'to appeal to the public in defence of the purity and excellence of their manufacture.'[20] Pamphlets were issued, letters written to influential newspapers and MPs lobbied in parliament; all the trappings in fact, of what we would today recognise as a professional and well-organised PR campaign by a special-interest group. When they started this there were 28 distillery companies in Ireland. By 1906 there were four.

Do we really want to repeat that process? Could Scotch possibly be blinded by today's golden glow and fall into the danger of believing its own seductive publicity myths? We're making great whisky, possibly as good as has ever been drunk.

Let's promote the merits of today's whisky: by relying on authenticity we might just be flying by the seat of our pants.

NOTES

1 See http://www.bruichladdich.com/the_history_ 2000tonow.htm
2 See http://www.morrisonbowmore.co.uk/ReadMore.aspx
3 See http://www.bruichladdich.com/the_distillery.htm
4 Alfred Barnard. *The Whisky Distilleries of the United Kingdom.* London: Harper's Weekly Gazette, 1887.
5 *Ibid.*
6 See http://www.bruichladdich.com/the_academy.htm
7 Joe Pine & James Gilmore. *thinkAbout Times.* Aurora: Strategic Horizons LLP, 2008.
8 Aeneas MacDonald (*pseud.* George Malcolm Thomson). *Whisky.* Edinburgh: The Porpoise Press, 1930.
9 The author can recall seeing open wort refrigerators in use in Devenish's Weymouth Brewery on entering the brewing industry in 1975.

10 Philp, JM, 'Cask quality and warehouse conditions' in JR Piggott, R Sharp and REB Duncan (Eds), *The Science and Technology of Whiskies*. Harlow: Longman Scientific and Technical, 1989.

11 Sir Walter Gilbey. *Notes on Alcohol*, London: Vinton & Co., 1904

12 Tasting or smelling of burnt organic matter (OED).

13 SH Hastie, *From Burn to Bottle*, Edinburgh (?): Scotch Whisky Association, 1951. As an official publication of the SWA, this presumably represented the prevailing industry view.

14 See http://www.defra.gov.uk/corporate/consult/whisky-regs08/whisky-draftsi.pdf

15 See http://scotlandonsunday.scotsman.com/whisky/ Distiller-sees-red-over.4186679.jp

16 JA Nettleton. *The Manufacture of Whisky and Plain Spirit*. Aberdeen: G. Cornwall & Sons, 1913.

17 SH Hastie, *From Burn to Bottle. Op cit.*

18 King James Bible. 1 Kings, 18:44.

19 William Chillingworth, *The Religion of Protestants: a Safe Way to Salvation*. Oxford: printed by Leonard Lichfield, to be sold by Iohn Clarke under St Peters Church in Corn-hill, 1637.

20 John Jameson & Son, *et al. Truths About Whisky*. London: Sutton, Sharpe & Co, 1878.

CHAPTER FIVE

MY FRIEND, WHISKY

John Hansell

'He's asleep. Let's go,' Alan said to me, as we quietly peeked into his family's living room. Alan was my high school buddy. His mother worked evenings. His father, like clockwork, would fall asleep every night in front of the TV. Normally, we would just spend the evenings hanging out in his bedroom, listening to music. But on this particular night, we had other plans. Alan told me about whiskey decanters his parents kept on the top shelf of their kitchen cabinet – unlocked and already opened.

Sneaking past the living-room and into the kitchen, I watched while Alan climbed up on the counter-top and opened a cabinet door. There they were; five of the most beautiful Wild Turkey decanters you would ever want to see. He brought one down from the shelf, quietly pulled the cork, and took a swig. Then he handed the decanter to me. I took a big sip. I felt the fiery amber nectar glide down my throat and warm my body.

Suddenly, Alan's father coughed. He woke up. We then heard him get up and change the channel on the TV. Alan quickly took the decanter over to the kitchen sink, added some tap water, put the stopper back on, placed it back up on the shelf and closed the door. We casually got a snack to eat and went back to his bedroom to listen to more music.

Getting to know you

That's the first time I remember drinking whiskey, but, as my mother would confess to me decades later, it wasn't the first time

I *drank* whiskey. She blames herself for introducing me to whiskey – when I was about six months old. I had begun teething and she wanted to give me something for the pain. She read somewhere (or so she thought) that giving me a shot of whiskey would ease the pain, so that's what she did. I'm sure it helped – and then some. She later learned that she was supposed to rub my gums with the whiskey, not give me a shot of the stuff. My father always said that I was such a happy child. Now I know why.

Speaking of my father, my parents divorced when I was about four years old. After that, I only could see him on Sundays. Dad was 'Mr Clean.' He was proud of the fact that he never drank, smoked, or swore. I learned that the pendulum could swing just as far in the other direction. My mother soon remarried. My earliest memory of my stepfather was of him sitting in front of the TV on Saturday mornings watching cartoons, cursing, smoking Phillies cigars and drinking Schlitz beer – all the things I never saw my own father do.

With my mother's new marriage, I suddenly inherited two older stepbrothers and two older stepsisters. I quickly discovered the dark side of alcohol. My elder brothers were both alcoholics and were regularly taking illegal drugs. Jim, the youngest one, crashed his car and broke his neck. He wore a body cast for six months and lived at home with us. He later drove into a police car, paralysing the policeman. A few years later, the officer committed suicide.

My mother recently told me that he was either drunk and/or on drugs during both of these incidents. His driving licence was revoked for the rest of his life. Now, after two broken marriages he is still an alcoholic and not in control of his life. The only reason I know he's still alive is because he calls my parents occasionally, usually drunk, asking for money. My other stepbrother Dan, while drunk, drove head-on into a telephone pole and killed himself. Several passengers were in the car with him; two of them were also killed. Dan may have survived his stint in Vietnam, but he lost his battle with alcohol.

Fortunately, throughout my life, not once have I ever 'needed' a drink. I have seen first-hand what an alcoholic is, and I am glad that I am not one.

Admiration

Sometimes you can know someone for years before becoming their friend. That's how my relationship with whisky began. Years passed. I moved on with my life, graduated from college, got a good job as a scientist, and married Amy, my college sweetheart. I was the only member of the family who went to college and got a good job. I made my parents proud.

During this time, I drank mostly beer, not whiskey. Back in the 1980s, you basically had a choice: fresh uninspiring beer or imported beer that was often old and stale. I decided to make my own beer which was fresh and flavourful, and I had a great time doing it. Every batch I made was a different style. For the first time in my life, I saw alcoholic beverages in a different context. They could be something with flavour, variety and intrigue. They were something I wanted to explore and get to know better.

In 1990, Bruce, the best man at my wedding, showed up one night at my house with a bottle of Johnnie Walker Black Label. He said it was to celebrate our ten years of friendship. We had never drunk whisky together before, and I had never tasted Scotch. Bruce unscrewed the cap and poured each of us a measure in two tumblers. I smelled the aromas. I tasted the flavours. I was impressed. At that moment, I became a Scotch drinker. Indeed, I became a whisky drinker. I had been drinking whisky for over a decade, but I was finally prepared, both mentally and emotionally, to enjoy it. The evening continued on, of course, with a few more confirmatory drams.

The very next morning, after Bruce left, I was glancing through my new issue of *Business Week* magazine. As fate would have it, in the 'Personal Business' section, there was an article on single malt Scotch. It explained that, even though it cost more than blended Scotch, it was worth it. Inspired, I drove to our local wine and spirits shop. There were only three whiskies: Glenfiddich, Laphroaig and The Glenlivet. I bought all three and so began my lifelong exploration of whisky.

But before I got very far, I ran into the same problem many newcomers to whisky encounter – how to drink it. I can honestly say that I knew I *should* like Scotch before I actually *liked* Scotch. I experienced the variety of flavours, the individuality, the quality etc, but wasn't fully enjoying it. I tried just about everything – ice, seltzer, mixers, water. I ultimately realised that it wasn't the flavours in the Scotch that I struggled with, but rather the alcohol. I was not used to the burn. I was a beer drinker. I thought imperial stouts were strong. The alcohol in whisky was four times that, and more.

I kept adding water to the whisky until it was so diluted that I didn't mind the alcohol and was able to appreciate the whisky's flavours. For me, it was an epiphany. I was now able to enjoy something that I admired and respected. I felt like I had found a new friend.

At the time, I was in a great position to enjoy whisky. There was a glut of whisky in the late 1980s and early 1990s. Prices were low, but you had to know where to find it. Most retailers throughout the US only had a small handful of single malts, but there were whisky 'goldmines' out there if you had the good fortune to be near one or had the inclination to seek them out. Some speciality whisky retail shops had dozens, if not more than a hundred different whiskies, most of them from independent bottlers.

I would travel on business as a scientist and my strategy when visiting a new city was always the same. This was before the Internet and its search engines. I would go to our local library and look up the speciality spirit stores in the yellow pages for the city I was visiting. I did the same for brewpubs and speciality beer bars. After my workday was completed, I would take a cab to a whisky retailer or two, buy my stash of whiskies, and then celebrate my new acquisitions by dining at a brewpub.

I had another strategy, which drove my wife crazy. For years, when I went past a liquor store, I would always take a quick peek in. I was always hoping that somewhere hidden in the back, collecting dust, I would find a rare (and often inexpensive) whisky. This is exactly how I stumbled across a 12-year-old distillery bottling of Ladyburn in Soho Wines and Spirits in New York City. Although it was a wine shop they had a few shelves of whisky in the back. I found they actually had two bottles of Ladyburn, but I only bought one; it cost me $28. I foolishly told the store manager about the whisky when I was buying it. I'll never do that again. I went back the very next morning to buy the second bottle. It was, of course, gone.

Then there was my first pilgrimage to whisky Mecca – Scotland. For three weeks in 1991, Amy and I travelled throughout Britain. Most of the trip was in Scotland, and most of the time we were visiting distilleries and pubs with great whisky selections and, of course, we visited whisky outlets. Amy was a true angel, somehow putting up with stops at all those destinations.

During our visit to Scotland, Michael Jackson's *Complete Guide to Single Malt Scotch* really was just that. Actually, it was more like a bible to me than a guide. On Post-Its, I wrote down all his highest rated whiskies and stuck them on the inside cover of the book and I took it with me everywhere. My goal was to taste as many highly rated whiskies as possible while we were in Britain. Some of the pubs were full of them, lined up on shelves on the back bar and a dram was usually a bargain. For many of the whiskies, it would be my only chance to taste them – or buy them – as many were never released in the US. What I learned in those few weeks was priceless.

My biggest challenge was bringing all of my new 'friends' back home with me. It was the most whisky I had ever brought back from Scotland at one time: 14 bottles. I brought an empty suitcase with me for that purpose, along with sturdy carry-on luggage. People always ask me how I got past customs with all that whisky. It was easy – I never told them. I never even thought about it, to be honest. If I had been asked to pay the duty, I gladly would have.

Everyone shows their respect and admiration for things in different ways. At the time, I wanted a bottle from as many distilleries as possible. I was pretty successful. As I recall, I had one bottle of whisky from more than 120 different distilleries. I had dozens from demolished distilleries, like Ladyburn and Kinclaith. I think that Ben Wyvis was the only distillery I couldn't find. (I later realised that having these whiskies sit on my shelves and collect dust was ridiculous, so I began sharing them at whisky tastings I was hosting.)

Eventually, Amy made a comment about my 'drinking' collection, and rightfully so. She's a very tolerant person, but I was pushing the limit. One New Year's Day I made a resolution which I posted up on our refrigerator. I vowed to not buy a single bottle of whisky the entire year! I needed to do something. I needed to find a way to continue exploring my passion for whisky, and still keep the peace at home.

Making it formal

During this time, the craft beer movement was picking up steam. My passion for whisky didn't extinguish my first love: beer. More and more small breweries were starting up. I was able to take my enthusiasm for beer and ride the wave of new beers being introduced. In Pennsylvania you have to buy beer at a beer 'distributor' by the case. If I bought a case of new beer and found out that I didn't like it, I was stuck with 23 more bottles of the stuff.

So, I started a beer club. I got 23 friends together and bought 24 cases of beer. I mixed up all the beers in my garage so that everyone received a case of 24 different beers. (My case, naturally, was free.) After the first beer club shipment, I got a lot of questions about the beer from the club members. So, for the next shipment, I tasted all the beers before distributing them, and I wrote up a little newsletter with tasting notes, information on beer styles, beer appreciation, etc.

The first newsletter was two pages long. The second one was four. The third one ended up covering eight pages and I included a listing of the local bars and restaurants in the area and the beers they had on tap. I thought to myself, 'Why am I writing eight pages of beer information for 23 people?' I asked my boss who was also a beer club member at the time, if I could come into the office on a Saturday, with my own paper, and print extra copies of the beer newsletter. He let me do it. (From then on, his case of beer was free too.)

I gave the newsletter a name. I called it *On Tap*, taking advantage of the listing of the draft beer selection at local restaurants and bars. I dropped off copies to all the places I listed in the newsletter, and to the local beer distributors.

Within two days, I had calls from a restaurant and a beer distributor, telling me they wanted to advertise. I was stunned. I wondered if this hobby could actually pay for my beer. The next issue, I added more bars and restaurants to the newsletter, which gave me more places to distribute it, so I printed more copies.

Our closest big city was Philadelphia. For the next issue, we included the well-known Philly beer bars and drove down to the city in the evenings, dropping off copies in the places we listed. Parking was impossible, so Amy would just drive around the block until I came back out of the bar. *On Tap* was now 16 pages long and growing. The very next week I received a call from a local Sam Adams beer wholesaler. He said he had someone who wanted to speak with me on the line. It was Jim Koch, founder and CEO or the Boston Beer Company, makers of Samuel Adams beer. Jim told me he admired my grass-roots effort and wanted to be part of it. He took out a full-page advertisement on the back cover.

For the next issue, we expanded *On Tap* to New York City. It was now 24 pages long. Amy and I spent a weekend visiting bars and restaurants, taking cabs from one place to another. We picked up advertising from New York beer bars, which paid for all of our costs. We even started getting subscribers. We had mailing parties at home where my friends would get together with me for a Saturday and help us stuff magazines into mailing envelopes to send out to various bars and restaurants.

A publication was born.

My beer club members wondered what the hell was going on; so did my boss. I found myself making ad calls during lunch and breaks at work. I was hosting beer dinners, going to beer festivals, and doing whatever I could to get *On Tap* in the hands of beer enthusiasts. During all this, my passion for whisky kept growing. I wanted to read and learn more about whisky. I wanted to write about it, and I was frustrated by the lack of any drinks magazine covering whisky. There already were several beer and wine publications on the market, but they rarely wrote about whisky. I approached a few of them about writing about whisky, but they all declined.

I sat there, looking at my most recent issue of *On Tap*, when an idea suddenly came to me. What if I doubled the size of the publication, devoting a new section entirely to whisky? I wouldn't upset my beer enthusiasts, because I wouldn't be taking away any space from them, and I could cover whisky more than any other drinks publication. But I would need a new name for the publication. I'd outgrown *On Tap*. What is the common thread between beer and whisky? Malt! I would call it *Malt Advocate*.

But I found myself running out of time and lacking expertise. I knew nothing about publishing, magazine design, advertising, or distribution. And there's no way I could do all the writing by myself. Something had to give.

After gaining a BSc and MSc, and earning several professional certifications and achievements in my field during my 14 years of employment, I quit. With a small severance package from my employer, Amy and I took a leap of faith. We made several changes in a very short time. In addition to the name change, we made the magazine glossy. We went national. We got a magazine distributor to get us into the bookstores. I found a very talented budding designer (who happened to attend one of my beer dinners) to design the magazine, and I hired an assistant to help me with all the paperwork. I asked prominent whisky writers like Michael Jackson, Charlie MacLean, and Gary Regan to write for *Malt Advocate*. They agreed, even though I couldn't pay them a lot. Everything was coming together. I kept costs low by having low overheads. Our office was in our house and Amy had recently given birth to our daughter, Shannon, but she agreed to go back to work for a year to help make ends meet. It was a sacrifice I will never forget. (One year later she quit and joined me as my business partner.)

After the very first issue of *Malt Advocate*, I received a call from the US brand manager for The Glenlivet. He wanted Glenlivet to be on the back cover of the next issue of *Malt*

Advocate. Shortly after that we raised advertising from The Classic Malts. Others followed. Slowly but surely, the whisky industry began embracing our efforts.

As our business grew, we gradually phased beer out of *Malt Advocate.* It wasn't that I didn't want to cover beer, but there were several beer publications out there and there were none devoted to whisky. Within a couple years, we transformed *Malt Advocate* into a dedicated whisky magazine (with due respect and reference to beer, of course). We were the first independent whisky magazine covering all of the world's whiskies.

Despite our progress, I felt that we couldn't survive on solely *Malt Advocate*'s advertising and subscriptions. We needed something else. We had discussions with other parties about possibly doing a festival, similar to the beer festivals that were going on at the time, and maybe having well-known whisky writers like Michael Jackson host seminars. But we were initially hesitant to host a festival where dozens of whiskies would be poured freely, and I didn't want to go down the route of whisky experts giving seminars. To me, the true heroes of the whisky world are the master distillers and master blenders. They are the ones making the stuff. I want to hear *them* tell me about *their* whisky.

I then approached several people I respected in the industry, and they all told me it would fail. They said I should bring in the well-known experts, like Michael Jackson. Everyone knew Michael. Nobody knew the master distillers.

We ignored their advice and took the plunge anyway. We decided to create a whisky festival where all the companies throughout the world would come together for a common cause – to educate people and promote whisky. Our theme was 'meet the maker.' We wanted the person who made the whisky to be the one pouring the whisky, and we wanted seminars to be conducted by them, not whisky writers.

I don't think Amy or I slept for the entire month before our first WhiskyFest in New York in November, 1998. The stress was incredible. Nothing like this had ever been done before. We were betting our entire business – indeed our entire financial future –

on this one event. We had to commit to paying the hotel huge sums of money before we even knew if the whisky industry, or the consumers, would participate.

As most of you know by now, WhiskyFest was a huge success. It was great to see the likes of Jimmy Russell, Fritz Maytag, Iain Henderson, Elmer T Lee and Richard Paterson promoting their whiskies. We have since expanded the WhiskyFest concept to Chicago and San Francisco. Now, there are whisky festivals across the globe, and the master distillers and master blenders are rock stars.

Meeting the Parents

When I quit my job as a scientist to focus on *Malt Advocate* full time, I had to tell my parents about my rather drastic career change. This was going to be a problem. While I was still attending high school and living at home, my mother and stepfather found religion. Literally. And in a big way. Within a few years, they quit their jobs and became missionaries. It probably saved their marriage, but suddenly alcohol became the work of the devil. Because of their new, deeply religious faith, I never let them know about my little side hobby, which was then evolving into a career.

Excepting my wedding, I never drank in front of them. They saw me as the one in the family who had succeeded, gone to college and had a successful career. I was not like my two older stepbrothers, who had let alcohol and drugs ruin their lives. Amy and I sat down with them in their kitchen. I explained what we were doing and why we were doing it. My mom tried to be understanding, but was unusually quiet. My stepfather didn't say anything. That was it. Or so I thought. My mother later confessed to me that they were devastated. They actually sought counselling.

Over the years, my mother has softened her position. She tries to be understanding. I don't think my stepfather has ever accepted it.

Saying goodbye? (Part 1)

Just as our business was blossoming, I was invited to London to tour the McMullen's Brewery and pubs. It was a red-eye flight and I slept the entire trip. The whole time I was travelling around London, I had a pain in my right calf. I thought I had pulled a muscle carrying my luggage up the steps of the hotel where we were staying. When I returned home, I went to see my family doctor because the pain was so great. My doctor felt the back of my calf and told me to go immediately to the hospital. He told me that he thought I had a blood clot and, if left unattended, it could travel to my lungs and I could die. I went to the hospital. I did indeed have a blood clot, which had developed during the flight. I was hospitalised for a week; they put me on blood thinners to dissolve the clot.

Sure enough, while in the hospital, the clot travelled to my lungs. The pain was so great, I couldn't breathe and I almost died. A nurse put a good dose of morphine in my IV, reducing the pain, allowing me to breathe again. The clot eventually dissolved and went away.

When I was being discharged, my doctor told me that he was putting me on coumadin, another blood thinner, and that I would have to stay on it for at least six months. I asked him what my restrictions were during this time. He looked at me and said: 'No alcohol.'

No alcohol?

He told me that my blood needed to be thinned to a certain level to avoid any future clots and that alcohol would interfere with this and could be very harmful to me. He said if I wanted to be safe, I needed to give up drinking for six months.

I told the doctor that I drank for a living. I knew that I had dozens of whiskies and beers waiting for me to review when I got home, and in the coming weeks would be hosting several whisky dinners. I thought about it for a while, contemplating how this would affect my personal and professional life, when I came up with an idea. I asked the doctor, 'What if I picked a certain amount to drink every day for the next six months, and kept to that amount? Would that work?'

He told me that no one had ever asked him that question before. He said normally he would never even entertain the thought, but considering my unique circumstances, he would allow it, as long as we monitored my blood with frequent tests.

So for the next six months, I had exactly two drinks a day. Every day. Doctor's orders.

Saying goodbye? (Part 2)

About five years ago, Amy decided to train for a marathon. I had been a runner all my life, so I wanted to train along with her. A few weeks before the marathon, when we were running really long distances, I got a pain in my right foot. The diagnosis was *plantar fasciitis*, so I began to undergo physical therapy for the pain.

But something strange happened. Instead of the pain going away, it spread. I literally felt the pain go up my leg, and then go up my other leg, until most of my body was in pain. The best way to describe it is this way: if your nervous system had a volume control between one and ten, mine suddenly was a fifteen. Since nerves control muscle function and relay pain, I was having trouble with both. In some ways, it felt like all the injuries I had ever experienced in my life had come back all at one time.

My body felt like it was mysteriously shutting down on me. Visits to podiatrists and orthopaedists quickly changed to neurologists and rheumatologists. No one could figure out what was wrong. Our vacation plans changed to visiting specialists in New York, Philadelphia and beyond. I had every possible neurological test done, along with MRIs for just about every part of my body. All were negative, so I started getting more general diagnoses: Fibromyalgia, Reflex Sympathetic Dystrophy, Chronic Regional Pain Syndrome, etc. These were terms I had never heard of before, and they all had sad stories that went along with them.

Finally, after dozens of tests and visits to the doctor, a neurosurgeon I consulted told me that I had some sort of neurological disease but he didn't know what kind it was, how I got it, or what was causing it. For this reason, he couldn't do anything about it. When doctors can't cure your illness, they will often prescribe medication to treat and manage it. Many prescription medications are metabolised in the liver, which is why they advise against drinking alcohol while you're on them.

One neurologist who we trusted, told me he had a drug that would help significantly with my pain, but I couldn't drink alcohol while I was on it. He looked me straight in the eyes and said, 'You have a choice: the drug or your career.'

The drug or my career?

It wasn't an easy decision because, at the time, I was in extreme pain. But, I chose my career. I found ways to manage the pain without the drugs that would affect my ability to function or damage my liver. It wasn't easy. Fortunately, the pain is now at a manageable level to the point where most of the time it is just a nuisance.

Friends of friends

Good friends introduce you to new friends, and that is what whisky has done for me. It is my love and passion for whisky that got me into this business, but it is the people who I have met through whisky that have kept me in it. Whisky drinkers are fun people and, for the most part, some of the nicest people you will ever meet.

I don't have a whisky collection, but I do have what I call a whisky 'accumulation.' Some of these whiskies are for the sole purpose of drinking, and nothing more than that. I have a fair amount of these 'drinking' whiskies which I regularly enjoy.

However, I have another group of whiskies which I also drink, or plan to drink, that have a greater purpose. Over the past 20 years I have accumulated – and still accumulate – whiskies with a connection to a person or place. The whisky inside some of the bottles I have may or may not be all that valuable, but the memories associated with them are priceless.

I still have that empty bottle of Johnnie Walker Black Label that my best man Bruce brought over to my house and shared with me, opening my door to the world of whisky. Whenever I see that bottle, I am reminded of that evening and the great time we had together, and I wonder how different my life would have been if he hadn't done that. What if I hadn't been exposed to Scotch for another three years or five years? Where would my life be right now?

I have a bottle of The Dalmore Stillman's Dram 30-year-old given to me by Richard Paterson, Whyte & Mackay's master blender, with a note written on the box that it came in. Any whisky with a note from Richard Paterson is special, but this one is even more so. It says:

> 'This is a rare baby which as I explained was finished in a special *oloroso* butt for nine years which origi-nally contained the Dalmore 50 year old – the same whisky you shared with me when we met for the first time in Edinburgh. Please enjoy and let your mind drift back in time.'

It brings back memories of when I first met Richard, who was conducting a tasting for a group of American journalists in Edinburgh, including myself. He called me out of the crowd and made me do a shot of whisky to prove a point in his demon-stration. Then he told me that it was 50-year-old Dalmore. (Richard, if I had known that, I would have savoured it a bit more!) Richard is one of the most entertaining people in the industry, always full of surprises. That was the beginning of a very special relationship that I have had with Richard for close to 15 years now.

I have a bottle of the 1975 Caol Ila Manager's Dram that was bottled in 1990. Manager's Dram whiskies are special bottlings by Diageo, chosen by the distillery managers and available only to their employees. They are not sold to the general public. I was on a press trip to Scotland. There was a whole load of us on the bus. Campbell Evans of the Scotch Whisky Association looked after us during the trip. We stopped in Dufftown for a break and some sightseeing. We had 15 minutes. I walk into a small gift shop with various knick-knacks and there, in the display at the counter, was one bottle of whisky. Just one bottle of whisky. The 1975 Caol Ila Manager's Dram.

Every time I asked the nice lady behind the counter how much she wanted for it, she told me it wasn't for sale. I kept increasing my offer and she kept refusing. Meanwhile the entire company of my press colleagues was waiting outside the shop, along with Campbell. He was standing outside the bus, next to its open door, staring at me, his patience wearing thin. We were *very* late for our next appointment. I must have caused him a great deal of grief that day but I convinced her to sell me the bottle. Campbell and I are still friends. Campbell, I promise you, when I open that bottle, you will be by my side.

I have another bottle I keep with my bourbons that is inscribed, 'To my friend John,' and it is signed 'Booker Noe.' I was in Chicago with other writers attending a day-long seminar on the Jim Beam brands. Later that evening, a few of us went to an outdoor concert in a park. There were three of us, Richard Carlton Hacker, Booker Noe and me, sitting around a table, listening to the music. I was in good company. Richard is one of the leading experts on cigars, so he promptly proceeded to give Booker and me a beautifully aged cigar to smoke. Booker opened up a bag next to him on the grass and pulled out a bottle of Booker's bourbon. We smoked our cigars, drank our Booker's and talked for hours. Booker had so many stories to tell, all of them precious, and most of them hilarious. Before we left that night, Booker took out another bottle, signed it with the above inscription, and gave it to me.

Sadly, we lost Booker a few years ago. On the day he passed, I opened up that bottle and shared it with friends, as he would have wanted me to do, as I reminisced about him.

I have hundreds of bottles like these. Each one has a story with it, and each story reminds me of the friends I have made over the years. And the friends I have lost. I'll drink some of those bottles very soon. For others, I will wait for just the right occasion to open them.

That's okay. I know I can wait. The test of a true friendship is when you can go for a long time without being with them, and then pick up right where you left off, without skipping a beat. That's how I feel about whisky.

CHAPTER SIX

THIRTY YEARS OF AMERICAN BEER

Julie Johnson

The American beer landscape has transformed profoundly and permanently. The most telling evidence is not the proliferation of high-end beer bars and retailers, but in the changes at the other end of the market: in the roadside convenience store. At the 'c-stores' customers find gas pumps outside and a rudimentary selection of groceries and household items inside: bad coffee, snacks for truckers and coolers of beer. The beer selection is dominated by our biggest brands, but nowadays it is very likely also to include two of the best major craft beers in the United States: Samuel Adams Boston Lager and Sierra Nevada Pale Ale, plus Blue Moon, a Belgian-style witbier brewed by mega-brewer Coors.

In three decades, a revolution in American brewing has seen brewpubs, microbreweries and the craft styles they produce move from eccentric novelties to a small but disproportionately influential position in the US beer world and beyond. The 'mainstreaming' of craft beer has broadened the audience for new flavours, opened business opportunities for a new generation of entrepreneurs, and even shaped the beers brewed by our biggest breweries, as well as the way beer is marketed and sold.

Internationally, the United States has a reputation for beer that can be reduced to one name: Budweiser. Drinkers in other countries deride the iconic Anheuser-Busch brand – as well as the beers produced by the other two in our 'Big Three,' Miller and Coors – for its modest taste as much as its global ubiquity. American beer enthusiasts condemn BudMillerCoors, as the trio are mockingly called, for brewing practices that lighten the beer with the use of rice and corn adjunct grains: the suspicion is that these practices were undertaken in the name of cost-cutting only, although that is not historically correct.

In fact, the American pale lagers are the culmination of more than a century of brewing history, a response to unique cultural and social conditions. These beers swept away competing beer styles, established some of the earliest national brands and provided the American drinker with what he wanted: a crisp, consistent, affordable, low-alcohol beverage.

And, eventually, the pale American lagers created such a homogeneous beer culture that they paved the way for a new beer movement, and one that should rightfully be the reputation of American beer today. Easy for an American to say, of course, but much more convincing when it came from Michael Jackson, who observed 'American cities now offer a diversity of beer styles far greater than that to be found in any single European country.'[1]

Setting the Stage

Like our language and legal system, the drinking and brewing culture of the American colonies and, later, the newly independent country, were solidly English. Revolution was fomented in the taverns of Philadelphia over mugs of ale. George Washington, the first president, favoured porter. Thomas Jefferson enlisted the help of an English brewer to establish a brewery at his home, Monticello.

But in the 19th century, the source of immigration from Europe shifted east, bringing over four million German-speaking settlers. They not only brought their own brewing traditions with them but also established new brewing businesses in America at a time when the innovative light lagers of Bavaria and Bohemia were captivating European drinkers – as they soon would Americans. The Bohemian style, in particular, became the model for new American brews.

From modest beginnings, the German immigrant brewers

became the highly visible and very wealthy leaders of this new industry. The list of German immigrant brewers, the 'Bier Barons,' includes names that resonate in the industry today: not only Busch, Miller and Coors, but also Pabst, Schlitz, Stroh and Leinenkugel. By the close of the century, lager production had soared, and American ale brewing all but disappeared.

The phenomenal success of the new Bohemian-style lagers happened to coincide with the growing momentum of the Temperance Movement, a tradition older than the Republic itself. Indeed, in the previous century, Benjamin Rush, a Philadelphia physician and signer of the Declaration of Independence, championed the cause of temperance to the new country. Rush promoted the consumption of beer and cider, regarding these weaker beverages as the healthy 'temperate' choice, in contrast to the dangers of distilled spirits.

However, by late in the 19th century, 'temperance' in matters of alcohol meant not moderation, but complete abstinence, or teetotalism. Campaigning for a national dry law, the Women's Christian Temperance Union and especially the powerful Anti-Saloon League stressed the damage done to families, the domestic violence, and the impoverishment of children caused when men frequented saloons.

Despite the fact that most Americans did not support Prohibition, particularly in regions of the country settled by German and middle-European immigrants, the 'wet' forces were no match for the temperance alliances. The 18th Amendment to the US Constitution – the Volstead Act, which instituted national prohibition – was ratified in 1919. Over 1,900 breweries across the country had one year to change products or board up their businesses.

Anyone who goes to the movies has a mental image of what then followed. Prohibition, being largely a rural movement, was laxly enforced in the cities, where alcohol consumption was driven underground. Lawlessness and political vice flourished as criminal mobs fought for turf and profit. Clearly, the 'noble experiment' was causing more harm than good.

Slowly, many of the original supporters of Prohibition

changed their positions. Women who had worried about alcohol's effects on the family came to see violence and corruption as greater ills. Eventually, though, it was economic stress that drove the forces of repeal. When the Great Depression struck in 1929, the need for both jobs and government revenue was compelling.

After 13 dry years, Congress passed the 21st Amendment in 1933, repealing Prohibition. Around 750 breweries survived to resume brewing, but consolidation and the later hardships of World War II cut their numbers to one third of that.

The years without legal beer, or spent drinking 'near beer' doctored with a syringe-full of grain alcohol, had lightened the American beer palate further. In response, the national breweries brewed beers that were some of the lightest in the world, our modern pale lagers.

Micro Pioneers

By the 1960s and 70s, the number of breweries in the United States hit a post-Prohibition low. National beer brands were a mainstay of mass culture, with heavy television and radio advertising and sports sponsorships. For adventurous drinkers, imported beers offered some cachet: Canadian beer was erroneously thought to be stronger (because alcohol was measured by volume, not weight, giving Canadian beer a higher percentage and apparently greater strength than American brands) and dark beers of any description were generally limited to a few imports, largely German.

American consumers, then, had little exposure to any beers except the dominant pale lager style. However, three points of contact put otherwise insular drinkers in touch with the wider beer world. First, home-brewing had gained a large, if illegal following during Prohibition; it surged again in the sixties and seventies, underground but barely, fuelled anew by anti-corporate, countercultural sentiments that extended to mass-marketed beer. Next, military service took American soldiers to

European posts where they discovered the local beer. Finally, increased opportunity for travel afforded increasing numbers of better-off private citizens and backpacking students a similar experience. Many Americans may have come back from a tour of Britain complaining about 'warm, flat beer,' but for a few, it was a revelation in flavour.

Our domestic beer monoculture motivated a few individuals on both coasts to redirect American brewing in a new, exciting direction. In California, the man credited with launching the American beer 'revolution' got a ten-year jump on everyone else, and Fritz Maytag's story is slightly different from those who followed him. In 1965, Maytag was a graduate student in Japanese studies at Stanford University. On a visit to San Francisco, he learned that the Anchor Brewery, whose beer he enjoyed, was to close.

Founded by German brewers in the 1850s, the brewery had quenched the thirst of California gold miners with 'steam beer,' a unique lager beer brewed of necessity at warmer ale-like temperatures. The company had survived the San Francisco earthquake and Prohibition, but shrinking distribution had left its bank balance critically low.

Maytag had the advantage of being the grandson of one of America's leading appliance manufacturers, and so was able to purchase a majority share of the brewery. It would require his independent wealth and many years of hard work to turn the brewery around.

Although Maytag's inspiration was Anchor Steam Beer (a name the company has trademarked: other beers brewed today in the steam-beer style are referred to as 'California Common'), he soon turned his sights and research to traditional English beer styles. In 1972, he released Anchor Porter at a time when porter was dying in its homeland. Unlike the dark imported beers Americans were acquainted with, this was – and still is – a lush, chocolatey brew, with a burst of hops.

In 1975, Anchor produced Liberty Ale to commemorate the bicentennial of the ride of Paul Revere during the American Revolutionary War. It was an all-malt beer, unlike many of the beers Maytag had sampled in England, and hopped with Cascade hops, the piney, grapefruity – catty, some say – variety that would become the signature of West Coast brewing.

In borrowing from English brewing traditions, Maytag promoted beer styles and flavours that were otherwise almost unavailable to American drinkers. But by tweaking the recipes with an American hop variety that was largely unknown in England – and when known there, often widely disliked – Maytag set the pattern for other innovative brewers, whose credo became, 'Borrow wherever you like, but be beholden to no tradition.'

Maytag is one of craft beer's great antiquarians. He followed Liberty Ale in the same year with the first American barley wine, Old Foghorn, and launched Our Christmas Ale, which introduced American drinkers to the concept of winter seasonal beers. To this day, this beer is brewed with different spices every year, always a secret.

North of San Francisco, the country's first purpose-built microbrewery – as opposed to a resurrected regional brewery such as Anchor – opened in Sonoma in 1976. Its founder was Jack McAuliffe, one of those travelling servicemen whose taste in beer had been broadened during his stint in the military. The brewery's name, New Albion, referred to Sir Francis Drake's description on glimpsing the Northern California landscape, as well as being a nod to McAuliffe's time in Scotland where he'd first discovered the kind of beer he wanted to make.

McAuliffe, like most American craft brewers who followed, made ales including a pale ale, a porter and a stout. Since the craft beer movement was reacting against the American mainstream, and that entire industry had descended from German traditions, it made sense to explore ale brewing as an alternative. But there were other reasons. Turnover was critical for these young, cash-starved businesses and ales didn't tie up valuable tank space as long as lagers would. And, to be honest, the darker ale styles were much more forgiving of amateur blunders and lack of consistency. Flaws that would be blatant in a light lager could hide behind the bulk of a porter. At the worst, if a beer came out of the tank tasting very different from what was intended, an audacious brewer could always dub it 'Belgian.'

Financial problems dragged New Albion down, but Maytag and McAuliffe became the established role models of California craft brewing, one having demonstrated the viability of old, flavourful beer styles, and the other having created the first modern micro-brewery from the ground up. In 1980, they were the inspiration when two avid home-brewers decided to start their own brewery further north in Chico, California, and created a brand that is among the nation's leaders today.

Ken Grossman had learned about home-brewing while a youngster, watching a friend's father brew beer. He and Paul Camusi, a fellow bicycle enthusiast and home-brewer, bootstrapped their brewery, to be called Sierra Nevada, cobbling together brewing tanks from salvaged dairy equipment and adapting a Coca-Cola bottling line to fill their beer bottles. Into those bottles they put Sierra Nevada Pale Ale, a highly hopped (Cascade, again) but beautifully balanced beer.

Sierra Nevada Pale Ale became the progenitor of a new beer style, the American pale ale, inspired by the English original, but with the distinctive hop varieties taking the lead, and softer American malts taking a supporting role.

On the East Coast

Conventionally, the West Coast is portrayed as innovative, mould-breaking – and a little uncouth. The American East Coast, with its longer history, is thought to be more bound by tradition, and more incremental than revolutionary in its approach to change. The cliché certainly fits the early years of the craft movement, though not for long.

Defenders of the East Coast brewing tradition will proudly point out that craft brewing couldn't be revived in the East, because, they say, it never went away. Yuengling Brewing Co, the country's oldest extant brewery, founded in 1829 and now in the hands of its seventh generation, has continued making a porter and an ale – despite the company's German origins. The loyal Yuengling drinkers of Pottsville, Pennsylvania, call the flagship Yuengling brew 'Vitamin Y.'

A few other regional breweries – 'heritage breweries' as they are often called as opposed to the new 'craft breweries' – kept non-mainstream styles alive. Most notable was probably Ballentine's, the only India pale ale in the United States to survive into the 1970s. The brewery succumbed in 1972, just before the broader craft beer movement grew to a size that could have embraced their uniquely dry-hopped beer.

But the old regionals – and there are a number still thriving – stood slightly apart from the craft movement. Family-held companies, such as Yuengling or Matt Brewing Co in upstate New York, were products of the same immigrant wave that gave rise to Anheuser-Busch, Miller and Coors. Their bigger brethren had gone national and enjoyed huge economies of scale; these small survivors were the few who had beaten the consolidation trends by catering to the beer needs of their home communities and nurturing traditional ties, not bucking them. They competed with the national brands by staying under the radar. But when the craft beer movement arrived in the East, new companies turned their backs on 'business as usual.'

'Business as usual,' in fact, might have been Jim Koch's destiny. With a business degree from Harvard, the Ohio native could have stuck with a lucrative career in consulting. Instead, he exhumed a great-great grandfather's beer recipe, convinced the leading brewing chemist in the country and father of a multitude of successful brands to re-formulate the recipe, founded Boston Beer Co and launched Samuel Adams Boston Lager in 1985.

In the best spirit of guerrilla marketing, Koch hawked his new beer door-to-door to Boston bars, convinced that, if he could win over bartenders, they would win over the beer drinkers. And Boston Lager, a faithful Vienna lager flavoured with Saaz hops, won admirers. Not only was it fuller in flavour and beautifully perfumed, but the golden brew looked different in the glass, its drinkers standing out in a bar full of light lager sippers.

Partly because Jim Koch's beers became successful and visible, partly because Koch himself was such a canny promoter of his own brand, he became a lightning rod for criticism. Arguments boiled in beer circles over his use of contract breweries to brew his beer. Could he be a 'craft brewer' if his beers weren't brewed at a brewery he actually owned? This was perhaps the first of many arguments over who could or couldn't wear the badge 'craft.' Was craft beer about beer style and flavour, or was it about the setting in which the beer was produced? If the former, Koch was a leader; the latter, he was out of the club.

The issue of contract brewing was seized upon by Anheuser-Busch in a very public campaign to discredit Koch in the name of 'truth in advertising.' Boston Beer may have been the prime target, but the campaign was meant to make the drinking public suspicious of the new craft brands in general – an early sign that the big brewers had noticed the small, significant changes going on around them.

In addition to flagship brand Boston Lager, the Sam Adams line helped introduce American drinkers to seasonal brews – one of the most popular trends in the market. In addition, Boston Beer's success has also allowed the company to support a line of highly experimental, principally high-alcohol beers, culminating in Utopias, the strongest beer in the world at some 26% alcohol by volume, which sells for over $100 per bottle.

This is the point at which to draw a line under individual brewery descriptions, because there are too many to credit, and because their stories, while singular, have common threads. With few exceptions (notably Dan Carey of Wisconsin's New Glarus Brewing Co), founders of American craft breweries came to brewing via home-brewing, not a professional background in brewing science. Almost all were men, most had trained for and begun careers in other areas, which ranged from civil engineering to broadcasting – in short, this was the era of the amateur.

The View from the Rockies

As new breweries were emerging on both coasts, the Rocky

Mountain state of Colorado gave birth to a movement that would both track and shape American beer drinkers' tastes. In 1978, shortly after President Jimmy Carter closed a long-standing loophole and legalised home-brewing, Charlie Papazian, a school teacher and avid home-brewer living in Boulder, formed the American Homebrewers Association (AHA).

The AHA, through its meetings and publications, forged connections between home-brewers, educating them and elevating their craft, and opening the door for entrepreneurial hobbyists to 'go pro.' It is no accident that the entrepreneurs who opened the vast majority of American microbreweries and brewpubs were home-brewers with other careers who 'went pro,' rather than technically educated brewers.

In 1982, the AHA hosted an event that would eventually give the growing ranks of microbrewers – who lacked the budgets or even the desire for conventional marketing methods – their most effective bridge to their public, the boldly-named Great American Beer Festival (GABF). 'Great' was a stretch: the first festival pulled together a small collection of microbrewers (of the few hundred that had opened by this point) and a couple of hundred fans in a hotel ballroom in Boulder.

As the GABF grew, later relocating to nearby Denver, it expressed and promoted a uniquely American attitude to beer, one focused almost obsessively on beer style and diversity. As evidenced by the spats over contract brewing and what consti-tuted a craft brewer, there was no 'right' way to brew in this new world. The craft brewing revolution started with a blank slate, almost completely cut off from any earlier American brewing traditions.

Brewers freely borrowed from every established European brewing heritage. A single microbrewery might offer a pale ale, a stout, a doppelbock and a fruited wheat beer. What's more, the brewer might add Munich malt to the English-derived pale ale, and spice the doppelbock with Kent Goldings hops. The fasci-nation was, simultaneously, a fidelity to old beer styles and an irreverent tinkering with those styles.

So, visitors to the GABF were confronted with a bounty of

beer styles, and encouraged to sample one or two ounces each of the greatest range of beers, rather than drink large amounts of a single style. This approach clearly separated the GABF, and the huge number of American beer festivals that have adopted the same model, from European beer events such as the Great British Beer Festival or Oktoberfest, which are primarily beer-drinking rather than beer-tasting occasions.

Early in its history, the GABF added a professional beer judging that would lend additional support to the festival's mission of educating beer drinkers in the diversity and quality of the new beers. The AHA and its younger sibling, the Association of Brewers, a Papazian-led professional organisation for micro-brewers, were the guardians of the growing list of beer style descriptions.

In the world of beer taxonomy, there are splitters and lumpers, as there are in any system of categorisation. The list of approved styles for the GAFB competition represents the splitters' school, with the number of styles proliferating over the years to more than 70. European brewers are often amazed, even dismissive, being accustomed to competitions with far fewer groupings. Yet the finely partitioned categories reflect the fasci-nation American brewers have had with the beer styles they have both borrowed and shaped: there is English IPA, for example, but there is also American IPA – a new and distinct style. The two can't be evaluated by the same criteria.

Not surprisingly, Michael Jackson was a hero to the emerging American craft beer community. His *World Guide to Beer* in 1978 became the home-brewer's encyclopaedic wish list of unfamiliar styles to tackle. Jackson travelled the States extensively, visiting most of the new establishments as they opened. His enthusiasm for the great variety of beer seemed to ally him more closely with eclectic American beer fans than with beer consumer groups such as Britain's CAMRA, which was more preservationist in its attitude and mission.

The commitment to beer style fidelity is apparent in the goal of the GABF competition, which seeks to recognise 'three world-class beers that best represent each beer style category as described and adopted by the GABF.' The style guidelines are quite rigid, setting out the desired appearance, aroma and flavour of each style, along with acceptable ranges for original and final gravities, bitterness, alcohol content and colour. Very good beers can fail to make any headway in the competition because they do not adhere faithfully to style.

But, despite GABF style guidelines, tastes and fashions change, as the evolving list of styles vividly shows. Hop-besotted American brewers boosted the bitterness and alcohol levels of their India pale ales beyond any acceptable technical specifications, until an entire new style, double or imperial India pale ale, was instituted with, again, its own rigid set of characteristics. This year, as brewers look farther afield for inspiration, the obscure Leipzig gose has just earned its own judging category, together with fresh hop ale, an American creation, and American Belgo-style ale, a dual-nation hybrid.

The Shakeout

By the 1990s, enough of these enterprises had succeeded to attract the attention of more speculative investors. If the first wave of micros was founded by entrepreneurs who dreamt of offering beer drinkers new options, the second wave attracted people who couldn't see beyond the novelty of small-scale brewing. Beers with quirky names and offbeat labels proliferated, and then failed when the beer itself didn't measure up. Confused consumers retreated to imported beers with more reliable reputations. It seemed no one had noticed that consumers' standards and knowledge had risen.

Observers clucked over the closures in the microbrewery 'shake out' and many saw this as a sign that craft beer had merely been a fad that had now faded. But, in reality, the business failures weeded out those breweries that made inferior beer or those that couldn't run a solid business. The survivors could do both, and craft beer started gathering momentum again, a mature and durable niche. Despite their small piece of the market, craft styles had become familiar to American drinkers. These were the styles that were written and talked about, that appeared at beer-themed dinners and in newspaper food sections. With the biggest craft brands widely available at even the most pedestrian bar, patrons weren't surprised to see more selections on tap than the brands from the Big Three. The beer revolution had become permanent.

Generational Change

By the turn of the new century, the founding craft breweries were celebrating 15 to 20 years of business. At some, including Sierra Nevada, Oregon's Rogue Ales, or Pennsylvania's Stoudt Brewing Co, the founders' children were old enough to begin taking a role in the business, an echo of the legacies of the bier barons.

At newly founded breweries, it became possible to spot a generational change in the new start-ups and the beers they chose to brew. The first generation mastered India pale ale, the next generation ramped it up to create the double IPA; the first generation revived porter, the next put dark chocolate and coffee beans in it; the first generation had to impress upon a naïve public that beer could be a high-quality beverage; the next one borrowed a corked-bottle format from the Belgians and demanded a place on the menu at white-tablecloth restaurants.

The past several years have become known for so-called 'extreme' beers, a term some resent for its connection to extreme sports and other recreational excesses. Whatever the name, the new innovations are a niche within the craft beer niche, encompassing the beers that most aggressively test our expectations about what beer really is. 'Beer geeks' have enthused about extreme brews that push the upper limits of alcohol or bitterness. The press has been intrigued by the high price extreme beer can command. Beer gourmets have embraced styles that challenge wine's primacy at the dining table. And brewers themselves are experimenting with rare ingredients and unconventional brewing techniques.

The most visible of the extreme set is probably Sam

Calagione, founder of Delaware's Dogfish Head Craft Brewery. In the best tradition of craft, he started his brewpub with a motley ten-gallon brewing system so small he was forced to brew almost around the clock. To stave off the boredom of repetition, he tinkered endlessly with his recipes, brewing with unusual ingredients including raisins, St John's Wort, chicory and cloudberries.

Calagione also looked beyond the usual sources for inspiration. In 2001, the Archaeology Department of the University of Pennsylvania applied techniques of modern chemical analysis to the remains of the presumed funeral feast of King Midas, excavated half a century earlier in what is now Turkey. They discovered that the king had been sent to his rest with a good supply of a brewed beverage. The analysis identified barley, grapes, honey and saffron and the researchers asked Calagione to brew a celebratory beer with those ingredients. The beer, Midas Touch, became an expensive but regular offering from the brewery and won Calagione a flood of press attention.

Dogfish Head is probably best known for its series of India pale ales in escalating strengths. Sixty Minute, 90 Minute and 120 Minute IPA achieve their hop character from doses of hops added every minute during brewing, for the respective lengths of time. The 120 Minute clocks in at a formidable 20% alcohol by volume.

On the other coast, another brewer took lessons from his background in wine. Vinnie Cilurzo of Russian River Brewing Co in Northern California devotes an impractical amount of his brewery space to the aging of beer in wooden barrels retired from use by spirits and wine makers. Cilurzo varies the base beer, the barrel source, and the micro-organisms to create complex, labour-intensive beers. He leads the new pack of brewers in creating Belgian-inspired (no longer Belgian-style) beers, inoculated with the *Brettanmyces* and *Lactobacillus* micro-organisms associated with Belgian lambic and sour beer, and aged in barrels of various provenances.

A number of other microbreweries are experimenting with wild-style fermentation and wood-aging, to such an extent that both are now reflected in the arbiter of beer styles, the GABF judging guidelines, codified as Wood and Barrel-Aged Beer, and Wood and Barrel-Aged Sour Beer.

Reaction from the Big Brewers

Craft beers own about five percent of the American market by volume – but more than that by sales, due to their higher price. At a time when mainstream brewers' products were stagnant or losing sales, the craft corner was growing by seven, then nine, then 12% per year. Trying to stem their losses, the big brewers couldn't help but take notice.

For more than a decade, the big American brewers had sought out stakes in craft breweries, with Anheuser-Busch buying into West Coast craft brewers Widmer and Redhook in exchange for the small breweries' access to A-B's uniquely powerful distribution network. The thinking, from the corporate point of view, was that if retailers indicated a demand for craft-styled beers, A-B would be able to fulfil that demand in-house, through its own craft-like brews or its partner breweries.

The other two in the Big Three took slightly different approaches. Miller Brewing Co, already the most removed from a family-owned brewing tradition, acquired a reputable family regional brewery in the form of Wisconsin's Leinenkugel. Insular Coors created its own craft branch, Blue Moon, which became a long-bubbling 'overnight success' with its Belgian witbier-styled Blue Moon Ale – which consumers generally identify as a craft beer, not a product from a mega-brewery.

Contrary to beer geeks' assertions that the big brewers make terrible beer, the big companies in fact employ highly skilled practitioners who make beer to exacting standards. The question, at a time when some consumers appear to be drawn increasingly to hand-crafted or artisan products, is not whether the big players can brew beer in more challenging styles, but whether they know what to do with it, and whether the beer drinker is looking for diverse flavour – which the big brewers could provide – or a craft beer sensibility, which they can't.

Looking Ahead

The modern story of new American beer starts with a fresh model that challenged the concept of national brands and the uniform national beer style. American brewing emerged from domination of our beer culture by a single European tradition that grew before Prohibition and consolidated its hold on the American palate afterwards. The reaction against that tradition launched a renewal of local brewing in styles that had been largely exiled from the country since the 19th century. These new companies, that we now take for granted as part of our current beer landscape, are writing their own history of American craft beer.

If the modern tale of American craft beer is really an unfolding tour of beer styles adopted and adapted, we can delineate the English Era (1978–1990), the Raspberry Wheat Era (1990–1995), the Belgian Aspirational Era (1995–2002), and the Wood and Wild Microbes Era (2003–present) – with variations along the way, and no doubt more to come.

What is clear is that craft beer in the United States is the most vibrant craft beer culture in the world, both derivative and creative, borrowing from traditional beer cultures and inspiring them in turns, and generating new directions in beer styles that will continue to surprise and delight.

NOTES

1 The Beer Hunter Online, July 2002.

CHAPTER SEVEN
THE RENAISSANCE
OF MALT WHISKY

Charles MacLean

Shortly before he died, Dorling Kindersley, publisher of Michael Jackson's renowned *Malt Whisky Companion*, commissioned him to produce an up-dated edition, the sixth. They required tasting notes for 1,500 malts. For the first edition of this book, published 18 years earlier, Michael managed to muster tasting notes for 122 malts bottled by their owners and 104 bottled by independents.

Is this not a striking illustration of how the market for malt whiskies has grown in two decades, measured by their availability? And if we look back a little further, the enormity of the growth in interest and availability really comes into focus. In this article I hope to explore this phenomenon, and to consider Michael Jackson's contribution to it. My approach will be from a literary perspective: I will examine in some detail the references to malt whisky made by earlier writers, filling this out from trade listings (principally *Harper's Wine & Spirit Gazette*) and company histories. At the same time I intend to touch on the broader market context for malt whisky and the market forces which have contributed to its success.

The Pre-history of Scotch malt whisky

Single malt whiskies – usually referred to as 'single whiskies' or 'pure malts' – were scarcely known outside Scotland until after World War II. Very little was offered for sale by the bottle, and that which was, was almost invariably bottled by independent wine and spirits merchants, not by the distillery owner. In some cases, distilleries were prepared to sell 'in bulk,' by the cask or stoneware jar, to such merchants, licensed grocers, hotels, pubs and private customers, sometimes (as with Glen Grant Distillery) providing paper labels which might be over-stamped with the bottlers' names. Such bottles from the early 20th century as have come to auction over the past 20 years bear witness to this.

The leading independent bottler of malt whisky – then and now – was Gordon & Macphail of Elgin, founded in 1895. From the outset, G&M bought new-make spirit from local distilleries and matured it in their own casks – at each individual distillery until 1960, when they built their own bonded warehouse in Elgin. Most of the mature whisky went into the firm's blends, but small amounts were bottled as singles.

Following the deaths of the founding partners in 1915 the firm passed to John Urquhart, who had started as a traveller[1] in 1895. When he brought his son and daughter, George and Betty, into the business in 1933, the former began to develop the malts side of the business, particularly after 1960, as we shall see.

The 1920s and 1930s

Aeneas MacDonald writes categorically that no bottled single malts were available in 1930,[2] although some could be acquired from individual distilleries. He mentions a bakers' dozen by name, his list expanding that of his former tutor, Professor George Saintsbury,[3] ten years before (see Table 1 opposite), which presumably were all bulk goods.

As I have said, 'bulk sales' of malt whisky were the norm in these days, but you generally had to have a friend with contacts to secure them if you were not in the trade. During the 1920s my grandfather was buying quarter casks of Glenmorangie with friends and bottling by hand. Their contact was a colleague who had formerly been a GP[4] in Tain. Lord Elgin remembers that his father had a cask of single malt in his cellar at Broomhall, near Dunfermline, from which the butler filled decanters or bottles

Table 1

	George Saintsbury (1920)	Aeneas Macdonald (1930)
Ardbeg	•	•
Ben Nevis	•	
Caol Ila	•	•
Clynelish	•	•
Glen Grant	•	•
Glenburgie		•
Glendronach	•	
Highland Park		•
Lagavulin	•	•
Linkwood		•
Longmorn		•
Macallan		•
Smith's Glenlivet	•	•
Talisker	•	•
Total	9	12

(readers will remember that 'butler' derives from 'bottler'). The distinguished Scottish judge, the late Lord Cameron who was born in 1900, told me that his father kept a cask of Islay whisky in his cellar, 'for drinking out of doors.'

In 1923 Matthew Gloag & Sons were offering five-gallon casks of *The Famous Grouse* to the general public with the sales line 'a cask gives greater satisfaction than can ever be got in bottle' for £18-10/-, ten gallon casks for £36, refills at 70/- per gallon [that's £3.50 in new currency], 'carriage paid on two gallons or more.'⁵

The only single malt I know of that was actively promoted by its owner in the USA was The Glenlivet. As soon as Prohibition ended in 1934, Bill Smith Grant began to look for business partners and shipped a few hundred cases; by 1939 shipments had increased nine-fold, including stocks of two-ounce miniatures for the Pullman Railway Company and Blue Ribbon intercity express trains.

The Post-war Decades

The demand for blended Scotch which followed World War II was equalled only by the 'Whisky Boom' of the 1890s. The problem confronting the industry was how to meet this demand. In 1945 stocks of mature malt whisky were at an all-time low – the output of the wartime years was equal to one year of pre-war production – and grain continued to be rationed until 1953. Mature whisky was at a premium, and there was certainly none available for single malt bottling.

In 1950 J Marshall Robb wrote: 'Nowadays, blends form by far the greatest proportion of whisky sales; in fact a large number of pure malts called self whiskies are not put on the market in the bottle in the pure state.'[6] Next year, Sir Robert Bruce Lockhart was 'regretting the passing of single pot-still malt whisky.'[7]

As soon as money was available, and assisted by measures such as the Manufacture of Spirits Regulation 1945 (which allowed distillers to mash, brew and distil concurrently), existing distilleries were expanded and modernised and 25 new ones built between 1949 and 1975. The output of malt whisky doubled, but the world's thirst for blended Scotch took up the surplus: between 1960 and 1970 exports tripled.

Harpers Directory and Manual for 1963 lists well over 2,000 Scotch whisky brand names of which only 30 are malts registered to the distillery owners, and three more registered to Gordon & Macphail (Linkwood, Mortlach and Strathisla). The same number is listed by Professor RJS McDowall in 1967, although some were 'difficult to find,' and it is not clear which of these were bottled by the proprietor and which by independent bottlers. George Urquhart introduced the Gordon & MacPhail Connoisseur's Choice range in the mid-60s.[8] Two years later another professor, David Daiches, listed 27 malts[9] – again, sometimes with qualifications: Bowmore 'only available at the distillery,' Old Pulteney 'rare,' Bladnoch 'not yet generally available,' etc. (See Table 2 below).

Table 2
Malts listed by Harper's Directory, RJS McDowall and David Daiches.
• = Proprietor's bottling
G&M = Gordon & Macphail independent bottling.

	Harpers 1963	McDowall 1967	Daiches 1969
Aberlour-Glenlivet		•	•
Ardbeg	•		•
Aultmore (n/a in London)		•	
Balblair		•	•
Balvenie		•	
Blair Athol		•	
Bladnoch (n/a as •)		•	
Bruichladdich (local pubs)		•	
Bowmore (distillery only)		•	
Cardhu (after 1965)		•	•
Clynelish	•	•	•
Cragganmore	•		
Dailuaine	•		
Dalmore	•	•	•
Dufftown-Glenlivet		•	•
Edradour	•		
Fettercairn	•		
Glencadam	•		
Glendronach	•		
Glenfarclas (• and G&M)	•	•	•
Glenfiddich	•	•	•
Glenforres-Glenlivet	•		
Glenfyne	•		

	Harpers 1963	McDowall 1967	Daiches 1969
Glenglassaugh	•		
Glen Grant	•	•	•
Glen Keith	•		
Smith's Glenlivet	•	•	•
Glen Mhor		•	•
Glenmorangie		•	•
Glen Moray	•		
Glenrothes-Glenlivet	•		•
Glen Scotia		•	•
Hazelburn	•		
Highland Park (G&M)	•	•	•
Imperial	•		
Lagavulin	•		•
Laphroaig	•	•	•
Linkwood	G&M	•	•
Littlemill	•		
Longmorn		•	•
Macallan (-Glenlivet to 1968)	•	•	•
Mortlach	G&M	•	•
Old Pulteney (rare)		•	•
Rosebank		•	•
Royal Lochnagar	•		
Springbank		•	•
Strathisla-Glenlivet	G&M	•	•
Talisker	•	•	•
Tamdhu-Glenlivet	•		
Tomatin		•	
Total	32	31	27

But things were about to change. As early as 1963 the directors of William Grant & Sons, all descendants of the founder, resolved to bottle Glenfiddich as a 'pure malt' ('straight malt' in the USA).

It was launched the following year, was soon to be found in the nascent 'duty free' shops in European airports and was being advertised nationally. The company's policy was to 'encourage drinkers to regard it as a natural extension to their experience of blended whisky … To add Glenfiddich to his repertoire for special occasions and personal enjoyment' (John Mole, UK Marketing Director). Sales of the brand rose by 50% in both 1970 and 1971.

Other distillers looked on with interest, some expressing open scepticism – notably the Distillers Company Limited (DCL), although its subsidiary, John Walker & Sons, began to bottle Cardhu in 1965, and was advertising it by 1969 with the line 'Cardhu single Highland malt Scotch whisky demands an educated palate.'

The 1970s

When Wallace Milroy joined his brother Jack in The Soho Wine Market in 1970, the shop stocked only four malts: Glenfiddich, Glen Grant, The Glenlivet and Tomatin. 'That was the norm then,' Jack recalled, 'There was some Laphroaig around, but they didn't want to sell it. Blends were the thing. Wallace decided we were going to have more malts. So he started scouting around.'

'We used to ask the reps from DCL for single malts and they'd say '"we don't do them." So we decided on a bit of blackmail. We'd say we'll buy *x* cases of your blends if you put five cases of the malts in. If they declined, they didn't get the order for the blends. At that point they'd usually reveal that there was some malt bottled for the directors' boardroom.'[10]

In truth, interest in malt whisky was stirring by the mid-1970s. Hugh MacDiarmid, the eminent Scottish poet, wrote in 1974: 'Only a few years ago it would have been useless to ask for a malt whisky in most of the English bars and even in Scotland, south of the Highland Line. Quite recently it has become a very different story. I had occasion recently to do a lot of motoring in the Upper Tyne valley, and in all the little pubs I visited, patronised by only a few shepherds and gamekeepers outside a little tourist traffic in the season, I found that every one stocked malt whiskies, and not just one of them but several, so that customers could choose which ones they wanted. Even more surprising to me was the bar in the Student's Union of a north English university, where I found between thirty and forty malts available.'[11]

The previous year the Edinburgh writer and journalist, Albert D Mackie, published what its dust-jacket described as 'the first popular book for the ordinary drinker who enjoys his dram.'[12] (See Table 3 opposite) It certainly provides an intriguing list of 'available single malts' – 64 expressions from 55 distilleries, although, again, some were 'difficult to get.'

Notwithstanding this, in 1974 bottled malt sales moved up by 69.49% in volume to 700,000 gallons, while value advanced by 51.95% to £4.24 million. Proprietors were beginning to follow William Grant's lead, albeit still in a small way, and with limited promotional support.

The independent distillers were first in: Macallan is a benchmark example. As early as 1963, their Chairman, George Harbinson, reported that 'the sale of Macallan in bottle is gaining momentum with a steadily increasing demand for the over 15 year old from the south of England,' and again in 1965: 'the interest in single malts is undoubtedly increasing and larger sales are expected.'[13] One year later Messrs Fratelli Rinaldi of Bologna were appointed sole agents for The Macallan in Italy, and following an advertising campaign, the following year they 'ordered more whisky than the total amount which went towards the home market.' Agents in France were appointed three years later.

The company's 1972 annual report noted that 'sales of cased Macallan had doubled during the year,' and added, prophetically, that 'a large increase in this type of business was anticipated in light of a fantastic growth in public interest, which would eventually see malt whisky becoming extremely fashionable.'[14]

The directors decided to conserve stocks of mature whisky, even at the expense of demand from their blending customers, and to 'put larger proportions aside for selling in cases.' But the demand for fillings meant that the company was not able to hold

Table 3
Malts listed by Albert D Mackie

	Expression/ availability	Independent bottlings
Aberlour-Glenlivet	8-y-o	
Ardbeg	8-y-o	
Auchentoshan	•	
Aultmore	12-y-o	
Balblair		•
Balvenie	11-y-o	•
Bladnoch	coming back	
Blair Athol	8-y-o	
Bowmore	•	
Bruichladdich	•	
Caperdonich	8-y-o	
Cardhu	12-y-o	
Clynelish	12, 15-y-o	
Dalmore	12, 20-y-o	
Deanston	not widely available	
Dufftown-Glenlivet	8-y-o	
Glen Garioch	•	
Glen Grant-Glenlivet	5, 10, 15-y-o	
Glen Ila (Caol Ila)	export only	
Glen Scotia	not widely available	
Glenburgie-Glenlivet	•	
Glendeveron	5-y-o	
Glendronach-Glenlivet	•	
Glendullan	12-y-o	
Glenfarclas-Glenlivet	8, 12-y-o	
Glenfiddich	8-y-o	10-y-o
Glengoyne	8-y-o	
Glenmorangie	12-y-o	
Glenrothes-Glenlivet	10-y-o	8, 20-y-o
Glenturret	not widely available	

	Expression/ availability	Independent bottlings
Highland Park	•	
Inchgower	12-y-o	
Isle of Jura	since Aug 1973	
Lagavulin	12-y-o	
Laphroaig	10-y-o	
Linkwood	12-y-o	
Littlemill	scarce	
Longmorn-Glenlivet	•	
Macallan	15-y-o	
Miltonduff-Glenlivet	•	
Mortlach	•	
Oban	•	
Old Fettercairn	•	
Old Pulteney	•	
Ord	•	
Rosebank	•	
Springbank	12-y-o	
Strathisla	•	
Talisker	8-y-o	
Tamdhu-Glenlivet		Wm Cadenhead
The Glenlivet	•	
Tomatin	•	
Tomintoul-Glenlivet	recently available	
Tormore	10-y-o	
Tullibardine	10-y-o	

55 distilleries in total	64 expressions	

back enough for its own use, so it was imperative that the distillery's production and maturation capacity was expanded. Seven stills had been added to the existing five in 1965/66, and following the sale of 35% of the company's shares on the Stock Exchange in 1968, further expansion was possible, so that by 1975 the total number of stills had risen to 21.

In 1978 Macallan appointed its first marketing director, Hugh Mitcalfe, who had moved across from Glen Grant following Seagram's takeover of that company, and who had been responsible for the tremendous success of Glen Grant in Italy. The year he arrived, the entire promotional budget allocated to The Macallan amounted to £50.

In 1979 Atkinson-Baldwin became UK agents, and in April 1980, Holmes Knight Ritchie (a leading London advertising agency) was appointed. Macallan offered a 10-year-old and an annual 'vintage' at around 18 years old (the first was from 1963). UK distribution was limited to specialist shops, but as soon as 'adequate distribution' was achieved it was planned to mount a consumer advertising campaign: HKR came up with a 'whispering campaign' of 24 small ads on the crossword pages of *The Times*, *The Scotsman* and *The Glasgow Herald*, with 'copy especially written to appeal to academics' and illustrations by Sara Midder and Angela Landels. The whole proposition 'fitted well with the slight "cult" tendency which surrounds the malt whisky drinker and these whiskies [i.e. the vintage idea] could be collector's items in the making.'[15] How prophetic!

Glenfiddich's UK Marketing Director, John Mole, remarked succinctly in 1980 that 'the main reason why more single malts are now being marketed lies in the steady success of Glenfiddich since the early 1960s.'[16] While this is undoubtedly the case, there is more to it.

As we have seen, the output of malt whisky doubled between 1945 and 1975, and the amount of whisky being held in bond more than quadrupled, to well in excess of a billion gallons. During this period, worldwide sales of Scotch grew at a compound rate of about nine percent per annum, higher than that of any other UK exporting industry. But in 1975 there was a severe slump, prompted by the oil crisis and end of the Vietnam War (which had stimulated the US economy). In Europe, the large and powerful supermarket chains began to demand lower prices.

The downturn encouraged amalgamation, led by brewers and overseas distillers, like Seagram and Pernod-Ricard. It was rumoured in the Stock Market that all independent whisky companies might be taken over. The increased involvement of powerful multinationals in the whisky industry, combined with the drop in demand for blended Scotch in the US, reduced the number of customers for fillings at a time when many distillers had recently expanded their production capacity. The case of Macallan, detailed above, was not atypical, and like Macallan, many independent distillers began to bottle and promote their malts as singles.

Around 1970, William Grant & Sons launched Balvenie as a single malt in the same innovative triangular bottle used for Glenfiddich and adopted from their Standfast blend. It was re-packaged in the equally striking 'vintage champagne' bottle in 1982. Arthur Bell & Sons introduced Blair Athol and Dufftown (both at 8 years old) in 1972, and added Inchgower 12-year-old in 1975. Also in the same year, John Dewar & Sons, part of the DCL, launched a 12-year-old Dewar's Pure Malt before replacing it with Glenordie from the Ord Distillery in 1983.

Whyte & Mackay did the same with Dalmore, Tomintoul-Glenlivet and Old Fettercairn around 1978, 'concentrating their [marketing] efforts in small special regional campaigns.' Glenfarclas appointed Saccone & Speed as agents in England and Wales in May 1979, 'concentrating on the on-trade.' Highland Distilleries launched Highland Park in September that year as a 12-year-old and repackaged Tamdhu 10-year-old while stating that 'In the very near future Bunnahabhain is expected to be marketed overseas.'

Laphroaig 10-year-old and Tormore 10-year-old, at that time both owned by Long John International, were 'freshened up' in 1979. Invergordon Distillers did the same with Bruichladdich and Tullibardine that year, and made plans to 'strongly advertise these malts to the trade' in 1980.

The 1980s

In the late 1970s *Decanter* magazine began to publish an annual supplement named *Harrod's Book of Whiskies*. The editor of both was Tony Lord, and in his introduction to the fourth edition of the supplement (1981), he remarks:

> 'In 1981 Scotch whisky means blended whisky.
> Only one bottle in a hundred is malt, the original
> whisky … Sadly only about half [of 120 distilleries]
> are bottled as single malt whiskies, and many of
> these are in such miniscule quantities as to be almost
> unobtainable.
>
> 'As recently as ten years ago [1970] only about
> thirty malts could be bought as singles, but fortunately
> the rapidly increasing appreciation of single malts
> for their individual character has seen this number
> nearly double.'[17]

In 1978 sales of single malt whisky accounted for less than 1% of the world market for Scotch, however demand both at home and abroad was growing faster than even the industry anticipated. In 1980 a symposium of whisky companies estimated that exports of single malts would rise by 8% to 10% per annum in the coming five years. In fact growth was twice that and continued to remain steady at around 10%.

There were two reasons for this: popular demand and availability. By 1980 the production of malt whisky had far outstripped demand. Scotch was no longer fashionable in the USA – the leading export market since 1939. Both here and in the UK the competition from vodka and white rum was stiff, and there was a large increase in wine consumption, actively encouraged in the UK by the government. In 1984 duty on wine was reduced by 20% to comply with an EC ruling on harmonisation, while that on spirits was increased by nearly one-third in five consecutive budgets (1979-1985). Inevitably, many blenders cut their filling orders, and distilleries began to close.[18]

In such a recessionary climate, one ray of hope for distillers was to offer their mature product as single malt. There was certainly no shortage, indeed, the 'whisky loch' of the early 1980s is still meeting the demand for very old malts, as singles or in super de-luxe blends.

And what of popular demand? We have seen how this increased during the 1970s. Another interesting measure is the number of books on the subject that appeared during the decade – publishers stand or fall by having a nose for subjects likely to interest readers. The 1970s produced around 30 titles – twice the number of books about Scotch published between 1950 and 1970, and three times the number of whisky books published 1900-1950.[19] This would increase dramatically in the 1980s and 1990s.

In spite of this clear interest in malt whisky, the trade was generally sceptical. Since the 1880s, the fortunes of the whisky industry had been based on blended Scotch, and traditionalists within the industry were very reluctant to see malt as more than a flash in the pan. Not least among those reluctant to put promotional money behind malts were the directors of the DCL, in spite of its blended brands suffering more than most in the hard market conditions of the time.

DCL did make a somewhat half-hearted attempt to get on the band-wagon in 1982 when it launched 'The Ascot Malt Cellar' – Ascot was the company's home trade base – a collection of four single malts and two vatted malts: Rosebank 8-year-old, Linkwood 12-year-old, Talisker 8-year-old, Lagavulin 12-year-old, Strathconon vatted (from James Buchanan & Co) and Glenleven vatted (from John Haig & Sons). They made little impact, but the selection of the malts, as representing regionally different styles, was to become highly significant after the Distillers' Company was taken over by Guinness in 1987.

Blenders had long discerned differences in the styles of malt whisky coming from various parts of Scotland, and their lists typically divide malts into 'Highland,' 'Lowland,' 'Islay' and 'Campbeltown.' A handful of writers had remarked on regional styles, Aeneas Macdonald going so far as to suggest ten sub-divisions for 'Highland,' and a further ten for what we now know as 'Speyside' (I can find no reference to this denomination being used until the mid-1970s). But only Professor McDowall described regional flavour characteristics and the very few that attempt to describe the style of individual whiskies do so in vague terms.[20]

The first writer to focus on flavour was Michael Jackson; he was also the first to treat regional differences in a systematic way, sub-dividing Speyside by its rivers and dividing 'Highland' into Western Islands, Western Highlands, Orkney, Northern Highlands, Eastern Highlands and Midlands in his *World Guide to Whiskies* (Dorling Kindersley, 1987). He developed and expanded upon tasting notes in his first *Malt Whisky Companion* (Dorling Kindersley, 1989). See Table 4 overleaf.

The novelty and significance of this approach will be readily apparent in an era in which malt whisky was both more widely available and winning an increasing number of devotees whose first priority was what it tasted like.

The year after the *World Guide* appeared, United Distillers (the successor to the DCL following the Guinness takeover), chose six single malts from their extensive estate which best demonstrated regional styles, tastefully repackaged them and offered them to the on-trade as a set, mounted on a stand. The Classic Malts were: Lagavulin (representing Islay, as it had done in the Ascot Cellar), Talisker (Islands, also from the Ascot Cellar), Oban (West Highlands), Cragganmore (Speyside), Dalwhinnie (Central Highlands) and Glenkinchie (Lowlands).

The promotion that accompanied the launch of the Classic Malts focused on flavour, appreciation and education. Using the theme of regional differences championed by Michael, and using Michael himself to present the first video promotion of the whiskies, stressing their varying flavour profiles, the launch opened up the whole sector and laid the foundations for the 'Malt Revolution' that gathered pace in the 1990s.

Was it a case of 'Nature imitating Art'? Hardly, more a matter of being tuned in to what whisky consumers wanted in the late 1980s. But that in itself was no mean achievement!

Table 4
Comparison of malts listed from 1980 to 1989

HG = *Harper's Wine & Spirits Gazette* feature (February 8th 1980, pp19-29)
HBoW = *The Harrod's Book of Whisky* by Tony Lord (4th Edn., *Decanter*, 1981)
MWA = Wallace Milroy's *Malt Whisky Almanac*, 1987. This edition (second) did not show an independent bottling if a proprietor's bottling was available. The independent bottlings were listed on pages 116-7 of the book.
MWC = Michael Jackson's *Malt Whisky Companion*, 1989
● = Proprietor's bottling
■ = Independent bottling
Names in *italics* are expressions of the proprietor's bottling that appears directly above them.

	HG 1980	HBoW 1981	MWA 1987	MWC 1989
Aberfeldy			■	■
Aberlour			●	●
Ardbeg	●	●	●	●■2
Ardmore			■	■
Auchentoshan	●		●3	●3
Aultmore		●	●	●■
Balblair			●	●■3
Balmenach			■2	■
Balvenie	●	●	●2	●2 ■
Banff				■
Ben Nevis			■	■2
Benriach			■3	■
Benrinnes			■2	■2
Benromach			■3	■
Bladnoch			●	●■
Blair Athol	●	●	●	●
Bowmore	●	●	●2	●4 ■
Brackla			■2	■2
Bruichladdich	●	●	●	●■
Bunnahabhain			●	●

	HG 1980	HBoW 1981	MWA 1987	MWC 1989
Caol Ila			■	●■
Caperdonich			■2	■2
Cardhu	●	●	●	●
Clynelish		●	●	●
Coleburn			■3	■
Convalmore			■2	■
Cragganmore			●rare ■3	●■
Craigellachie			■2	■2
Dailuaine			■2	■2
Dallas Dhu			■2	■
Dalmore	●		●	●
Dalwhinnie			●	●■
Deanston	●		●	●
Dufftown	●		●	●2
Edradour			●	●■
Fettercairn	●	●	●	●
Glen Albyn			■2	■
Glenallachie			●	●
Glenburgie			●rare	■
Glencraig				■
Glencadam			■3	■2
Glen Deveron			●	●
Macduff			■3	■
Glendronach		●2	●2	●2 ■
Glendullan			●	●■
Glen Elgin	●	●	●	●
Glenesk		●	●	●
Glenfarclas	●	●2	●6	●6 ■
Glenfiddich	●	●	●	●4 ■
Glen Garioch		●	●2	●
Glenglassaugh			●	●■
Glengoyne		●	●3	●3

	HG 1980	HBoW 1981	MWA 1987	MWC 1989
Glen Grant	●	●	●2	●7 ■3
Glen Keith			■3	■
Glenkinchie			■	●■2
Glenlivet	●	●	●	●2 ■4
Glenlochy			■3	■2
Glenlossie			■3	■
Glen Mhor			■3	■2
Glenmorangie	●	●	●	●2
Glen Moray	●	●	●	●2 ■
Glenordie		●	●	●■
Glenrothes			■3	●
Glen Scotia		●	●	●
Glen Spey			●	●
Glentauchers			■	■
Glenturret			●4	●8 ■
Glenugie			■3	
Glenury Royal		●	●	●■2
Highland Park	●		●	●2 ■
Imperial			■	■
Inchgower	●	●	●	●
Inchmurrin			●	●
Inverleven			■	■
Isle of Jura		●	●	●■
Kinclaith			■3	■2
Knockando		●	●	●2
Knockdhu			■	■
Ladyburn			■	■
Lagavulin	●	●	●	●2
Laphroaig	●	●	●2	●2
Linkwood			●	●■4
Littlemill		●	●	●■
Lochnagar		●	●	●2

	HG 1980	HBoW 1981	MWA 1987	MWC 1989
Lochside			■2	■
Longmorn		•	•	•■3
Macallan	•	•4	•8	•5
Millburn			■2	■
Miltonduff		•	•	•
Mosstowie			■	■
Mortlach			■4	■2
North Port			■2	■
Oban		•	•	•2 ■2
Port Ellen			■	■
Pulteney			■3	■
Rosebank		•	•	•3
St Magdalene			■3	■
Scapa			■3	•2
Singleton			•	•
Speyburn			■2	■2
Springbank		•	•10	•2
Longrow			•	•
Strathisla			•	•■6
Talisker		•	•	•2
Tamdhu	•	•	•	•3
Tamnavulin		•	•	•■
Teaninich			■3	■
Tobermory		•	•	•
Ledaig			■	■
Tomatin	•	•	•2	•■
Tomintoul		•	•	•
Tormore	•	•	•	•2
Tullibardine	•	•	•	•

Total of 108 distilleries	•27	•49	•101 ■94	•122 ■104

NOTES

1 A sales representative, or travelling salesman.
2 Aeneas MacDonald. *Whisky.* Edinburgh, 1930. Reprinted by Canongate, 2006, p.117
3 George Saintsbury. *Notes on a Cellar Book.* London, 1920, p.79. His 'Notes' on Scotch whisky fill only four out of 166 pages.
4 General Practitioner. A doctor.
5 Mackie & Co. advertised their 1921 new make at:
   Lagavulin 6/3d per original proof gallon [i.e. 31p per 4.5 litres]. Malt Mill 6/4d, Craigellachie-Glenlivet 6/- and Hazelburn 5/6d – less 1d per gallon if the customers' own wood was filled, less a further 1d if the cask was uplifted immediately.
6 JM Robb. *Scotch Whisky, An Illustrated Guide.* Edinburgh, (1950), p.47
7 Sir Robert Bruce Lockhart. *Scotch.* (1951), p.169:
   'Personally I regret the passing of single pot-still malt whisky. I drink it whenever I can find it. But I realise that it is the nectar of the young and the strong, that it goes best with Highland air and long tramps over hill and moor, and that it is ill-suited to the man who sits all day on an office stool.'
8 RJS McDowall. *The Whiskies of Scotland* (1967)
9 David Daiches. *Scotch Whisky, It's Past and Present* (1969)
10 Quoted by Joanna Simon in *Whisky Magazine,* Issue 5, p.62. The 'boardroom malts' belonging to the DCL, referred to by Wallace Milroy, were probably: Clynelish (12yo @ 70° and 75° proof and 15yo @ 90° proof), Glendullan (12yo @ 82.3° proof), Glen Ila (from Caol Ila Distillery; export only), Lagavulin (12yo @ 75° proof), Linkwood (scarce @ 75° proof), Mortlach, Oban, Ord (@ 76° proof), Rosebank and Talisker (8yo @ 70°, 80° and 100° proof).
11 Hugh MacDiarmid et al, *Scotch Whisky.* London (1974), p.65.
12 Albert D Mackie. *The Scotch Whisky Drinker's Companion.* Edinburgh (1973).
   It is difficult to know whether they are proprietor's bottlings or independent bottlings, and there are some omissions (eg Dufftown-Glenlivet, launched at 8yo with Blair Athol 8yo in April 1972. Curiously, Inchgower 12yo, which he lists, was not introduced by Bell's until May 1975, two years after the book was published). One suspects he was more familiar with some makes than others. Please refer to Table 3.
13 John Frame. *Notes Towards a History of the Macallan Distillery.* (unpublished MS, 1999) p.104
14 Ibid, p.148
15 *Harpers Wine & Spirit Gazette.* 8th Feb 1980 (Special Whisky Report)
16 Ibid.
17 Tony Lord. *Harrod's Book of Whiskies. Decanter Magazine.* 4th Ed. 1981
18 Between 1980 and 1985, thirty malt whisky distilleries were mothballed, although 11 of these resumed production by the end of the decade.
19 These figures come from a whisky bibliography compiled by Ian Buxton in late 2005, a selection of which appeared in *Book Collector Magazine* Nov, 2006, pp.61–64.
20 Honourable mention must be made here of Wallace Milroy's *Malt Whisky Almanac, A Taster's Guide* (Lochar Publishing, 1986) and to John Lamond and Robin Tucek's *The Malt File* (Benedict Books, for The Malt Whisky Association, 1989), both of which included tasting notes.

CHAPTER EIGHT
A'BUNADH: A SHORT STORY

Hans Offringa

The door of the small white cottage opened, its hinges creaking and barely withstanding a fierce wind blowing from the north. In the gap appeared a tall, slightly stooped figure with a weather-beaten face. He had to bend in order to get out. Carefully Alan MacManus checked the old cask that stood just outside the doorpost. Satisfied, he turned and went inside again, pulling the door tightly shut behind his broad back. Half an hour later the wind died down and the sun broke through the clouds. MacManus reappeared, stepped outside, and walked to the bench that stood in front of his little house. He stretched his body, feeling the mild warmth of the late afternoon sun and sat down.

In the distance he could distinguish the contours of the distillery where he had worked as a cooper and warehouseman for more than 60 years. When eventually he had to lay down his labour, exceeding the retirement age by ten years, he was given the old oak cask as a present. Everybody at the distillery agreed he was the only one to claim it. It was not just *a* cask. Like its current owner it had served the whisky industry for decades, but its history seemed to go back much further than MacManus'.

He was approaching 80 now, but it didn't show. The sturdy Scot looked like a late 60-something, weathered but strong and healthy. The sea air, a daily dram and common sense had contributed to his long working career. After his wife died from a quick but nasty illness, he considered retiring. His sons, both working at the distillery, urged him to continue for a while, realising their father needed the distraction in a time of mourning. He had agreed.

The 'while' had lasted ten years, although MacManus did not move many casks during that time. Not that he was opposed to physical exercise. On the contrary, almost every day he took his bicycle and went downhill to the village of Glensporran by the Sea, heading to the distillery at the eponymous bay for a chat with his former colleagues. Sometimes he took a group of visitors on a tour and amused them with his knowledge and anecdotes from the near and distant past. Like the story of the cask.

The cask. MacManus looked at it again. How on earth was it possible? A small miracle! Again he peered in the distance to the distillery and his mind wandered, reminiscing about the curious tale. He was inseparably connected to the story. When he told visitors, they usually didn't believe him and filed the story under the heading 'urban legends.' Once in a while a single person asked after the tour if he could see the cask. If he liked the individual, MacManus would invite him to come to his cottage, striding beside him, bike in hand. A 45-minute walk.

One time a journalist took a picture of the cask and promised MacManus to write about it and send him a copy of the magazine in which it would be published. Either the man didn't write the article or simply forgot, since MacManus never received anything. A small number of people did come to the distillery and ask specifically about the cask. Apparently the legend had spread.

When had he first become involved in the cask story? That must have been more than 30 years ago. The then distillery manager, a remarkable character called Benjamin Lovett, took a special interest in wood maturation and wanted to know every-thing there was to know about American and European oak. MacManus grinned when he remembered a statement from his former boss, 'I want to understand everything about oak wood. I am prepared to go back to the actual acorn, if need be.'

At the time good casks were readily available, yet slowly but surely the contours of a future scarcity were sketched. Spain had stopped shipping sherry in casks to English and Scottish ports. Instead, bottling took place on the Iberian peninsula, leaving the casks at the bodegas. In addition the worldwide consumption of sherry continued to decrease. As a consequence ex-sherry casks were more difficult to obtain by the Scottish distilleries and the prices rose considerably. Ex-bourbon barrels were at hand in abundance, but usually required modification into the larger hogshead size. Regardless of the source, all the casks had to be inspected closely. After all good spirit could be ruined by maturation in bad wood.

One day Lovett had said to McManus, 'I want to investigate the places where the casks originally come from. What I really want is a hand in selecting the actual wood from which the casks are being made.' It didn't take long for Lovett to put his bold words into action; within a year he had managed to visit both Spain and the US.

In the former country he'd had long talks with the owners of several sherry bodegas, learning about the use and influence of European oak for maturing sherry. The visit to the latter country had been to view the largest cooperage in the US and to a lumberyard in the Ozark Mountains, Missouri. In both countries Lovett had come to a workable agreement. The bodegas were willing to specially prepare casks for him, which only seemed a logical thing to do.

His experiences in the US were far more exciting. The general manager of the lumberyard took Lovett to a specific hillside in the Ozarks and let him choose several trees. In time they would be cut down, sawn and turned into casks that would be marked and shipped straight to Glensporran.

'One of the trees was growing a distance away from the rest,' Lovett told McManus when he had returned to Scotland. 'Of course that was the one I chose but at first they didn't want to agree because of a story attached to that oak. The tree was supposed to have been planted by a Scottish immigrant who once worked at the lumberyard. The man said he wanted to become rooted in America. He visited the sapling every year to check on its progress because he was saving money to buy the land surrounding the tree as a home site. There was even a newspaper article written about it. According to local lore he never did get the land and went back to Scotland some 20 years after planting that acorn. It's our good fortune that the oak is only around 100 years old, a bit older than the usual age for cutting trees for barrels.'

At first MacManus had shrugged his shoulders at the tale. In the 19th century many, many Scots crossed the Atlantic in search of a better life. However, Lovett didn't want to hear any doubtful remarks. 'The story gets even better MacManus, since that Scot carried the same surname as you do. See? Here's the newspaper article.'

Lovett showed his surprised employee a photocopy. 'You see?' Alan replied, 'Do you know how many MacManuses there are in the world?'

Lovett smiled enigmatically and said as he left, 'Just wait and see. I will find out more!'

Five years after that remarkable conversation MacManus was called to accept a special delivery from the US. It turned out to be five casks. The accompanying papers described them as having been made from one tree, after which they had been seasoned with a special American whiskey for four years, according to Lovett's specifications. 'Those casks are made from the tree your forefather planted, old boy!' Lovett called out when he noticed the arrival of the shipment a day later.

Lovett certainly hadn't wasted any time between his first visit to the US and the delivery of casks. A request for intensive research in the Scottish and American genealogical and emigration archives brought something to light that even Lovett couldn't have dreamed up. The MacManus who had immigrated to the US and planted the oak tree in the Ozark Mountains never returned to Scotland. However, his eldest son James had. The latter had fallen out with his father after a bitter argument at the lumberyard where they were both employed. As a consequence James went back to Scotland, determined never to communicate with his father or siblings again.

His family tried several times over the years for a reconciliation, but the letters were returned to them in the States. As James had rigorously cut the family ties with America, his four sons never knew about their family on the other side of the Atlantic. But James' oldest son must have had his grandfather's genes because at the age of 18 he became a cooper's apprentice in lower Speyside. He married and had four sons too. One of them would later follow in his father's footsteps and become a cooper at a distillery in the Northern Highlands.

'See, you can't deny it, my man! The oak from this cask was planted by your great-grandfather.' Alan MacManus had looked at his boss in bewilderment, not believing a word he'd said.

Lovett responded, 'It's true. Letters sent to James MacManus were still in the possession of an American MacManus. Here in this folder are all the papers concerned.'

At home MacManus had told the entire story to his wife, still not fully convinced. Eventually the letters and Lovett's persistence changed his mind. On top of this he received a unique assignment. 'We are going to mature a very special whisky in those casks and I want you to personally take care of them until I decide to bottle the contents.' A responsibility MacManus couldn't possibly refuse. He chose the warehouse closest to the sea and reserved a special corner for the five casks.

Ten years later Lovett decided it was time to bottle the first batch. The taste was very special, a bit spicier and creamier than the standard 10-year-old Glensporran. At the launch of this newest expression Lovett said, 'The acorn, the place of origin, the cask seasoning, the time and the care all contributed to the MacManus-edition of our whisky.'

It became a tradition and over the next three decades, each 10th year a limited edition would be launched. After that time the casks would not be rejuvenated again. Four were resting in the warehouse, awaiting their final bottling in six years' time. The contents of the fifth one had been bottled for Ben Lovett's retirement some years ago. This cask now stood firmly beside the front door of MacManus' cottage. Almost 130 years old, the ultimate consequence of a deed performed by his great-grand-father: the planting of a little acorn on a sloping hill, somewhere in the middle of the USA.

MacManus suddenly woke up from daydreaming on his bench, hearing a clear, high voice, 'Hi Grandad, did you sleep well?' A 10-year-old boy threw his bicycle against the cask and ran to his grandfather. 'Hey, wee man, watch it with that cask. Later you will inherit it, so better be careful.'

'Why should I have it, grandpa?'

'Well, come and sit down, Michael.'

MacManus took a deep breath and commenced telling an old family tale.

CHAPTER NINE

A QUESTION OF PRIORITIES

F Paul Pacult

In the North American media of the late 1980s, wine was the white-hot subject matter of choice for consumer-oriented publications. Spurred on by excellent Bordeaux vintages in 1982, 1985, 1986, 1988, and 1989 as well as by the emergence of California as an exciting wine region, a full-tilt, fine-wine revolution was occurring in the US. By contrast, distilled spirits were considered, in editorial circles at least, as impolitic, passé and, therefore, journalistically radioactive. Libations like whisky, brandy and gin belonged, it seemed, to a generation on the wane.

During that period, I earned my crust as a contributing wine writer to several US-based lifestyle publications and as the sole operator of a wine school, Wine Courses International, headquartered out of a downtown Manhattan loft space. It was an exhilarating time to reside and work in New York, the American city that most enthusiastically embraced wine more than as a curiosity, but increasingly as a daily enjoyment.

Considering the wine-related hoopla, I remain grateful that I said 'yes' to a question involving Scotch whisky that was posed to me in the winter of 1989 by a *New York Times* executive. That question was hatched in the wake of one of my advanced wine classes, attended by 20 professional men and women bent on honing their wine-appreciation skills. Three of the course participants worked for the *Times*. At the conclusion of the class, the *Times* staffers, Rich Colandrea, Bob Haidt and Roger Schwoerer, approached me, hands extended. Over the course of our conversation, Rich mentioned that he and his colleagues had read articles that I'd written for *Wine & Spirits Magazine*. Then, out of the blue, came the question that forever changed the paths of my professional and private lives.

'Paul, how'd you like to write about Scotch whisky for the *Times* Sunday magazine?'

I still remember the shock of it. With the blood draining from my face, my weight shifting from one leg to the other, my arms folding across my chest snug as a straightjacket, I wittily stammered, 'Scotch whisky?' my voice trailing off like a stone thrown down a well at the word *whisky.*

Pivotal On-The-Spot Decision Time: Do I boldly fess up to Rich and his companions that I know as much about Scotch whisky as I do about performing triple-bypass heart surgery, possibly less? Or, taking the coward's route, do I suavely bluff my way through this situation because, after all, this *is* the *New York* which-is-why-I-came-to-New-York-from-California-in-the-first-place *Times* asking me to write for them?

As scores of friends and associates would doubtless testify to, suave and I mix as well as Scotch and peanut butter and fried banana sandwiches. Candour got the better of me and since I'd never been given trophies for sporting a poker face (and even if I had been nominated for such an award, the audience's doubled-over laughter would have told me all I needed to know) I admitted to Rich, Bob, and Roger my near-complete lack of familiarity with Scotch whisky, uttering feebly about it being 'a tipple from my parent's generation.' At critical moments like that, I used to resort to employing third-tier terms like *tipple* as a sort of deflection tactic, hoping that maybe the listener will mentally double-clutch while pondering the word, giving me more time to consider my options.

Rich didn't nibble at my bait as he calmly assured me that my acknowledged deficit of Scotch whisky acumen was acceptable and that I would be given ample time to conduct research. My wine writing background and knowledge, in their eyes, were plusses, not obstacles. They just, bless their everlasting souls, wanted *me* to write this 5,000-word special section, which would be supported by advertising, because they liked my wordsmithing skills.

Further, Rich explained, because their market research bore out that Scotch whisky might soon be on the rise and, to date, no nationally distributed US newspaper had ventured forth with such a project highlighting a non-wine adult beverage, the *Times* wanted to be the newspaper to break the new ground. The *Times* wanting to be the first major American newspaper to devote space in their flagship *Sunday Magazine* to an emerging topic that, in their view, wine-centric editors had heretofore failed to cover, appealed to me as much as getting the chance to write for the nation's foremost chronicler of events.

I finished hearing Rich, Bob and Roger out, taking note of their enthusiasm for the project and sensing somewhere deep in the recesses of my grey matter that this project might indeed work out well on all fronts. Nevertheless, at that first meeting I asked them if, considering that was I in essence a wine schlub, I could ponder their thunderbolt of a request for a day. Following a night of rumination and dreams of being chased down an alley by a frothing madman in a kilt named Angus, I called Rich the next morning and agreed to write for him.

'I'll work up the contract and courier it to your office. In the meantime, you prepare to go to Scotland to visit some distilleries, talk to some industry people, absorb the environment, eat some haggis, learn everything you can about Scotch whisky and come back by July with 5,000 words about Scotch whisky and Scotland. We'll hook you up then with the art director for this project. Get some photos. The magazine goes to press in late November and hits the streets on December 3rd with the Sunday newspaper,' summarised Rich. We agreed on a fair writing fee and with that Scotch whisky formally entered my life.

'We need a working title. What do you want to call this piece?' queried Rich. Scrambling, I blurted, 'Scotch Whisky – A Consumer Guide.'

'Good. That works. Travel safely,' wished Rich. 'Oh, and one other thing. Let's keep this project quiet for the moment. Don't want the competition hearing about it sooner than they need to hear about it.'

Hanging up, I thought, 'Visit Scotland? Outstanding. Bone

up on whisky? An exciting and new experience. Go to distilleries? Cool. Writing for the *Times*? Nifty ... but what's haggis?'

What occurred over the next several weeks went a long way in cementing my belief that I had correctly answered Rich's question. The closed, sniffy community of East Coast wine media somehow caught wind of my *Times* assignment. One of my colleagues claimed that she had heard rumblings that I was starting a new wine column for the Sunday magazine; others had caught wind of more accurate whispers that I had been hired to write about Scotch whisky or cognac or bourbon or liquor, booze, hootch, rotgut of some sort.

But it was when a senior member of the press corps, now deceased, confronted me about my mysterious *Times* assignment that I realised I had possibly struck the mother lode. I can still hear his words delivered in a forbidding hushed tone reminiscent of Father Ryan in the St Eugene's Parish confessional of my Roman Catholic childhood: 'Let me just say that writing about a *thing* like whisky won't do much to advance your wine writing career. Whisky is, is unfashionable and ... well ... brown.'

My unspoken reaction: thank you for your unintentional imprimatur. When I get back from Scotland we can share a bottle of Beaujolais or, better, a shot of *thing* ... even if it is ... brown. On second thoughts, don't expect a call.

First Impressions

In preparation for my inaugural excursion to Scotland, I read whatever few outdated books and materials were available about Scotch whisky in the spirits data desert of North America. Michael Jackson's first edition of *Complete Guide to Single Malt Scotch*, the book I really needed, wouldn't be available in the US until 1990. I learned soon enough that Michael was *the* journalistic voice of whisky and beer. In time, he and I would develop a cordial relationship based largely on sporadic meetings in wonderfully odd places, usually whisky festivals at which we would both be booked for speaking engagements and book signings, the Quaich Bar at the splendid Craigellachie Hotel in Speyside, or, best of all, at distilleries.

Looking back, I'm glad that there wasn't yet a surfeit of information on whisky because I believe that, consequently, I journeyed to Scotland in a more receptive and uncluttered frame of mind. I had few expectations and now, in 2008, I see that reality as a seeding of the fertile scenario that had, to my good fortune, unfolded at my feet.

In early May 1989 I travelled to Scotland, landing in Edinburgh by way of London. From New York, I had arranged to be assisted on my fact-finding journey by Yvonne Scott, the media liaison of the Scotch Whisky Association. This would mark the first of many trips to Scotland that would enrich the next 19 years in order to supply the scores of articles and columns I would come to write about Scotch, not just for the *New York Times*, but for numerous other publications.

It wasn't just the subtle power of the *New York Times* that opened the doors of Scotland for me; in the first three years of my research trips it was really Yvonne and her amazing list of contacts. Later on, it would be Campbell Evans and Tony Tucker of the SWA who made my yearly, sometimes bi-annual research sojourns so productive and enjoyably memorable as my writing about Scotch whisky and spirit in general became my primary focal point.

I remember my first trip well. Yvonne and I visited Glenlivet Distillery first. My memory of eyeing the distillery as we rounded a bend in the road is as crisp as the weather that clear morning. We also made stops at Linkwood, Glenrothes, Glenfarclas, Aberlour, Glenmorangie and Dalmore over the next three days. From the mainland we hopped up to the Orkneys for a brief visit to Highland Park. The distilleries of Auchentoshan and Fettercairn rounded out that initial excursion. Islay, Campbeltown, the central Highlands and the west coast would have to be saved for my next trip.

From that initial exposure, I recall immediately liking the floral smell of raw whisky as well as the grainy, snack-cracker aroma of the distillery complex at Glenlivet. The crystalline clarity of the virgin spirit coming off the spirit still through the spirit safe brought back a certain comment by a peer about whisky's brownness. I found that as much as anything I liked the nuts and bolts of distilling and the mysteries of maturation. Since I had worked at a northern California winery from 1973 to 1982, there was something noble and sturdy, to me, about the production process. All the shiny copper and steel and brass impressed me. Michael would later tell me at Highland Park in 1997, 'These are the events that matter most to whisky.'

But my favourite lasting snapshot from the first journey was being ushered into the bonded warehouses, in particular at Highland Park and Glenlivet, where the combination of cathedral-like tranquillity, damp coolness, and malty sweetness created a palpable environment that differed significantly from the wine cellars, Champagne caves, or sherry bodegas I had visited when wearing my wine-writer's hat. In these silent structures scattered around Scotland, that are typically surrounded by idyllic and verdant backdrops that are sometimes accentuated by the sound of rushing water, the air was permeated with aromas of cereal grains, baking spices, wood resins, and dried fruits. This on-site crash course was intoxicating in the finest usage of the word.

Tasting malt whisky from distillery to distillery highlighted in the most vivid way how remarkably individual each distillery's whiskies are and, for the most part, do not even closely resemble those of nearby neighbours. At Fettercairn Distillery in the south of Aberdeenshire, I learned about blending from the highly animated and impeccably attired master blender Richard Paterson. At Glenmorangie in Tain, the discussion focused tightly on barrel management, barrel selection and the critical importance of oak ageing. The enormity and complexity of the subject of Scotch whisky, from malting to mashing to fermentation to distillation to wood maturation, mounted with each distillery visit, with every conversation. Even a library of reference books devoted to whisky could not have prepared me for what I was experiencing on-site in Scotland.

Not only was I struck by the stunning elegance and depth of

the liquids that the hospitable and humorous natives, one out of three of whom seemed to be named Ian, called *whisky*, spelled without an *e* as it is in America, but I took a robust liking to Scotland itself. As a Chicago, Illinois native of Polish descent who'd lived in California and Hawaii before colliding like an asteroid with New York City, I felt inexplicably at home in the wilds of Scotland's Highlands. My comfort had something to do with the silence; something about the impossibly photogenic mountains and the fine needlepoint mist and the cattle in need of a trim and a shave; something about the sparkling rivers, streams, lochs, and the tranquil, orderly villages that moved me to want to write about Scotch whisky through the prism of Scotland and the Scots. It was obvious from the beginning that one aspect could not possibly be addressed without full inclusion of the others. This was unusually rich writing material that simply wasn't being told to Americans.

While I remained an ardent, card-carrying admirer and chronicler of wine, for that would never change, I felt a seismic jolt of creative eruption because of Scotch whisky that I had never before experienced as a journalist. Simultaneously, rather than being in awe or feeling intimidated by the subject matter of the *Times* assignment, I found that I was at ease with the entire immersion, in large measure due to the directness of the Scots, who to a person were welcoming and straightforward with their no-frills replies to my questions. They appeared to genuinely enjoy speaking about their industry, their whiskies and their craft. Many were, after all, third-, fourth-, fifth-generation workers at the same distillery who had learned the business from fathers, uncles and grandfathers. They told me no great trade secrets; they just worked hard, took pride in what they did and paid attention to detail.

Another positive factor was how Scotland's distillery workers addressed their competitors and their neighbours' whiskies in amiable and respectful words. The people at Glenlivet were friends with the people at Macallan who played football with the workers at Glenfiddich who were cousins or in-laws of the people at Glenrothes who drank at the pub with the guys from Speyside

Cooperage who were close mates with ... and on and on. The whisky industry people were organically connected.

Finally, in what seemed like a blink of an eye, I was bidding Yvonne goodbye at Edinburgh Airport. I didn't want to leave Scotland, yet I knew that I had to. There was work to do. And, I felt that I'd be back. I just didn't realise at that point how many times I would return. Yvonne's parting words were, 'Find a book by Michael Jackson. That'll help with your research.'

After returning to Manhattan, the story exploded from me in my office on First Avenue. Punctuation eluded me as the story flowed from my memory bank like water tumbling over Niagara Falls. Commas, semicolons and periods couldn't stem the tide. The words came in torrents, not sentences.

To provide perspective on how viscerally I reacted to Scotland and whisky on that initial trip, if you recall Rich Colandrea had given me the assignment of providing the *Times* with 5,000 words. When it came time for me to submit the copy in July 1989, he received 21 pages of manuscript blanketed with 10,000 words. A few days after handing over the story to Rich, I called him to query when he'd like me to begin editing the word-count down to a manageable 5,000 total.

'You kidding me? Don't even think about it,' said Rich. 'This story has been passed around and nobody wants you to cut a word. We're going to use all of it. You'd better get in here soon to meet with the art director, though. This thing is going to be massive ... much bigger than we ever conceived.'

I asked Rich about photography for the story.

'Try the British Tourist Authority office over on 57th Street. I'm told that they have a decent photo library of all things related to Great Britain.'

I did so, whereupon I met Sue Woodley, the BTA's photo librarian. Sue provided scores of print-worthy images and indeed the *Times* ended up using many of them.

On Sunday, 3 December 1989, the four-colour, 28-page special section called 'Scotch Whisky – A Consumer Guide' appeared in the Sunday magazine. The response from *Times* readers was, to my relief, overwhelmingly positive. Rich and the

Times were happy and within a couple of weeks he signed me up for two more *Sunday Magazine* stories in 1990, another Scotch whisky story and one on cognac.

In the spring of 1990, with unabashed glee I toured Islay, Jura and the central and western Highlands with Yvonne Scott. My other companion was my copy of Michael's *Complete Guide to Single Malt Scotch*. I relished comparing what whiskies I tasted at the distilleries with his notes on them. Even though it was keenly apparent to me that we had very different palates, I had to suppose from his beer background and mine in wine, his notes and insights provided a safe and reliable touchstone in my early years of whisky evaluations. Michael was erudite without being the least bit stuffy.

Following the success of the first *Times* Scotch section, importers of whisky and brandy and vodka and gin and tequila flooded my office with samples. Other magazines began calling, asking for short articles on spirits, mostly Scotch whisky. I still wrote about wine, but Scotch and spirits were gaining from the outside.

On the first Sunday in December 1990, the second *New York Times Sunday Magazine* with a special section on Scotch whisky hit the streets and by the next week I had a third contract for another Scotch whisky story for 1991 plus two more spirits assignments. It was as though a light switch had been turned 'on' and I was lucky enough to be in the room.

Lasting impressions

By early 1991, I was writing about whisky and spirits as much as wine. The demands for copy from editors likewise kept increasing in size. In 1990 the assignments would typically call for 200 to 300 words, then in 1991 they grew to 500 to 1,000 words. Because I was evaluating so many whiskies and others spirits that were being sent to my office, I kicked off publication of the subscription-only, advertising-free newsletter, *F. Paul Pacult's Spirit Journal.*

Scotch whisky, as *Spirit Journal* readers know, is my favourite spirits category and, as such, it commands much of the editorial coverage from issue to issue. I had no money to promote the *Spirit Journal* in 1991, still don't, and yet somehow 18 years later it continues to be published quarterly, with Scotch as its flagship topic.

Simultaneously, sales of Scotch in North America, Asia and Western Europe edged up through the early to mid-1990s as consumers, mostly red wine lovers, in my view, became fascinated with single malts. The consumer world was primed and aching for Scotch whisky. I'm convinced beyond any doubt that Scotch whisky's unique natural thumbprint, its accurate reflection of its place of origin even in many blends, is as much the cause of this interest as its inherent grace as a world-class libation. Serious wine lovers understood the concept of *terroir* and no other type of distilled beverage, except for cognac, could supply that much residue from its source environment as Scotch whisky. What made Scotch different from all other spirits was that it had Scotland.

As the world evolved from regional commercial sectors into the global network economy due to free trade, the revolution in electronic communication and, in general, peace, Scotch whisky proved to be the ideal beverage to lead the charge for distilled spirits. In light of the economic upswing from the late 1980s and well into the 1990s and consumers' tastes gravitating towards greater complexity, Scotch whisky answered the call as an international icon that hadn't lost sight of its roots.

And the growing results in sales, product availability and media attention have been astounding in scope. In 1989, perhaps one could find six to eight single malts on retail merchants' shelves in New York while today the number of distilleries represented might be 80 or 90 plus all the independent merchant bottlings. When all product line items are included from each distillery and the independents, meaning malts and blends of different ages or different wood finishes, the total roster of Scotch whiskies in many top-notch American retail stores surpasses 300, 400, even 500 items. This is how far Scotch whisky has come in the last two decades. From a brown thing that no one wanted to write about to a first-rate beverage that many journalists and publications now *need* to write about, just to keep pace with the competition.

I went on to write a total of 17 special Scotch whisky sections for the *New York Times Sunday Magazine* over the ensuing years. I've lost track of all the other articles I've written focusing on Scotch for other publications since 1989. I estimate that I've had published somewhere in the neighbourhood of between 350,000 and 450,000 words on Scotch. Twenty years on I acknowledge that I'm still just scratching the surface on what needs to be written about Scotch whisky. I find myself still in the position of discovery. And with each fresh discovery comes a fuller sense of awe and respect for the subject matter.

Invariably, with each new writing assignment or project on whisky I come back to the same seminal message that I unearthed in May of 1989 on my first journey to Scotland: that single malt, blended malt and blended Scotch whiskies are the greatest of all distilled alcoholic beverages and are the ones whose inherently complex natures unfold in greater degrees of depth, discovery and intensity with each tasting, with each nosing, with each dram, time after time. If there was ever a quintessential definition of the term *elixir,* Scotch whisky is it.

All along the way, Michael Jackson's peerless journalistic contributions and books have inspired and guided all of us who decided to further the cause and tell the story of whisky, not to mention the millions of whisky drinkers around the world who trusted him. Even today, with thousands of whisky reviews under my belt and Michael sadly gone too soon, I reach over to the whisky shelves in my office library and hunt down the last edition of Michael's *Complete Guide to Single Malt Scotch* just to remind myself what he thought about Highland Park 25 or Talisker 10 or Longmorn 15. He was, after all, the first of us. He was, after all, the foremost among us.

At the outset, I mentioned that a question about Scotch whisky had dramatically altered the course of my professional *and* private lives. On the professional side, it's been an honour to write about so vibrant a topic for so long and I hope that that aspect has shone through.

On the personal level, I courted and married Sue Woodley, the breathtaking woman at the British Tourist Authority who provided the images for that inaugural *New York Times Sunday Magazine* section. Sue is now my partner as well as the managing editor of the *Spirit Journal.*

Amazing how a single question can turn priorities upside down and, in the end, right side up.

CHAPTER TEN
LAGERING

Roger Protz

When Benedictine monks built the monastery of Weihenstephan at Freising near Munich in 790 they chose a hill to site their place of worship. They made the decision for sound defensive reasons – they could see their enemies coming – but they found, when they added a brewery in 1040, that caves beneath the monastery were ideal for storing and maturing beer. In common with other monastic brewers in the region – Munich is a corruption of *Mönchen*, the Monks' Place – they had a constant struggle to stop beer going sour during the long, hot summers. They discovered that beer stored in deep, cool caves was free from both summer heat and infection from wild yeasts. Stored beer enjoyed a long, slow secondary fermentation, with the yeast nibbling away at remaining malt sugars and finally settling at the base of the brewing vessels. The monks built on this empirical knowledge. They cut ice from rivers and lakes and packed the cellars with it to maintain a cool temperature during the summer months.

The German for a storage place is *lager*. The monks had discovered a new method of brewing and a new style of beer, lager bier. Weihenstephan monastery, or Holy Stephen, the first Christian martyr, was secularised in the 19th century. Ownership passed to the Bavarian royal family and, after World War One, was handed on to the government. The brewery, still state-owned, is today part of the brewing faculty of Munich University and enjoys international renown for the quality of its wheat beers and a superb Pilsner. Its beers carry the logo *Älteste Brauerei Der Welt* – the oldest brewery in the world – but few would demur if it called itself the oldest *lager* brewery in the world.

It's a common misconception that lager is a comparatively new arrival on the beer scene. The main reason for that impression is that lager is thought of as a pale, golden drink, a style associated with the beer that burst like a meteorite across the skies in 1842 from the new Burghers' Brewery in Pilsen in Bohemia (now part of the Czech Republic). German was the official language at the time and the beer was dubbed Pilsner – *of Pilsen.*

Beer from Pilsen was a sensation. It was taken by boat up the Elbe into northern Germany and from there into Scandinavia. A beer train left every day with supplies for Vienna where the capital of the sprawling Habsburg empire helped widen knowledge and desire for the phenomenal new style. The second wave of emigrants to the United States took with them the knowledge and ability to make golden lager and began to transform brewing in that vast country. Today, 93% of all the beer brewed in the world is lager beer and the majority of it is based – for better or worse – on the Bohemian style. The Burghers' Brewery renamed itself Pilsner Urquell – Original Source Pilsner – but few of its imitators live up to the brilliance of the template created in the middle of the 19th century.

But the success of Pilsner masked the fact that lagering beer had existed for centuries. In common with beer everywhere, whether ale or lager, it was dark in colour. Until the industrial revolution of the late 18th and 19th centuries, malt was kilned or cured over wood fires. The result was brown malt and brown beer. The great brewers of Munich – Löwenbräu, Spaten and Paulaner among others – stored their beers in deep cellars packed with ice but produced Dunkel Bier or dark beer: in common with industrial workers in England with a preference for sweet, dark mild ale, Bavarian drinkers preferred the malty and energy-restoring qualities of brown beer.

It was the invention of coke – coal that burned without emitting gases – that enabled brewers to make pale malt for the first time on a commercial scale. Martin Stelzer, the architect who designed the Burghers' Brewery in Pilsen, visited England and returned with a coke-fired malt kiln. It's an irony of brewing history that the inspiration for the original Pilsner came as much from English brewers of pale ale as the lager brewers of central Europe. But similarities between pale ale and golden lager should not be over-emphasised. Burton-on-Trent, the ancestral home of pale ale and its export version, India Pale Ale, stands on sandstone, as do Pilsen and another important brewing centre, Bamberg in neighbouring Franconia. If you attempted to dig deep cellars in Burton, they would immediately fill with water from the Trent Valley, which is one reason why the Burton brewers remained faithful to their warm-fermented style. In Pilsen and Bamberg, on the other hand, not only could deep cellars be dug but also the invention in the 19th century by Carl von Linde of ice-making machines meant that lagering no longer depended on ice from rivers and lakes. As a result, lager brewing moved from a seasonal activity to a regular one.

To see the origins of commercial lager brewing, following the collapse of monastic power, it is necessary – and it is a pleasant necessity – to visit Franconia, the northern region of Bavaria. Nuremberg is a city of great antiquity and ravishing architecture and they should not be overshadowed by the more recent, grim history of the Nazis and their rallies, held outside the city centre. Nuremberg is the birthplace of the Reformation and the artist Albrecht Dürer. His house stands opposite a small but fascinating brewery, the Hausbrauerei Altstadthof, which translates clumsily as 'the old town courtyard house brewery.'

Brewing dates from 1386 and the brewhouse stands above part of the labyrinth of cellars that runs under the city. The cellars and the city walls form part of the medieval defences of Nuremberg and for centuries the cellars have provided storage space for valuable artwork and perishables, including beer. Brewing at the Altstadthof stopped in 1906 but the historic link was restored in the 1990s by Reinhard Engel. He produces four regular beers: *helles* (pale lager), a red beer (*roth*), a black beer (*schwarz*), and a *weiss* or wheat beer. They are brewed in traditional vessels: a copper mashing vessel that doubles as the kettle, where the wort, or sugary extract, is boiled with hops, and a wooden filtration vessel known as the *lauter*. Both primary fermentation and lagering take place in wooden vessels in a cold room alongside the brewhouse. But when Herr Engel makes the Bavarian speciality, Bock, he stores them – May Bock and Double Bock – in the cellars for three months.

The origins of Bock beer lie in the north of Germany, in the former Hanseatic trading city of Einbeck. Its beers were called Einbecker and were taken south in the 17th century when the Duke of Brunswick married the daughter of a Bavarian aristocrat and beer was needed for the festivities that followed, festivities that were the forerunner of the world-famous Oktoberfest beer festival. The Bavarians enjoyed the strong beer and began to brew the style themselves. In the local dialect Einbecker beer became Einbocker, which over time was shortened to the simple, explosive Bock.

The most famous Bock beers were brewed by monks at the Paulaner monastery in Munich, which was not secularised until the 19th century. In common with Weihenstephan, Paulaner was built on a hill with deep cellars for lagering beer. It's an intriguing question: were the original beers from Einbeck warm-fermented – that is, a type of ale – as Lower Saxony lacks the hills and caves in which beer could have been stored prior to refrigeration, but became a lager bier when it moved south?

In the cellars at Nuremberg, Reinhard Engel stores not only his seasonal Bocks but also a special version of the style that is so strong that it needs a Champagne yeast to finish fermentation when conventional brewers' yeast gives up the ghost.

To witness traditional lagering in all its glory you have to make the short, 45-minute train journey from Nuremberg to Bamberg. This small city of 70,000 people is a UNESCO World Heritage site with half-timbered medieval buildings nestling alongside Baroque and Renaissance styles. It has eleven breweries – it once had many more – and the Benedictine monastery that looms above the city has a fine brewing museum in cellars where monks once lagered their beer. Bamberg is steeped in beer.

The first licence to brew was granted in 1122 and the city's own *Reinheitsgebot* or Purity Law – which permits only the use of malted grain, hops, water and yeast – pre-dates the Bavarian royal family's similar edict of 1516 by 26 years. In the early 19th century, Bamberg had 65 breweries when the population was just 20,000. The number of artefacts in the city – storage cellars, chimneys and lofts where malt was dried – suggests that centuries earlier there were possibly hundreds of tiny house breweries using communally-owned brewing vessels, passed from house to house. The city's beers include fascinating examples of *Rauch* or smoked beer, made from malt roasted over beech-wood fires. The method was once widespread in Europe and the British Isles until wood was replaced by coke.

The best known of Bamberg's surviving breweries is Heller-Trum. Its fame is due to the fact that it exports its smoked beer far and wide and also serves it on draught in the celebrated Schlenkerla tavern in the city centre on Dominikerstraße. Heller has been brewing since 1678. The brewery was first based in the tavern but moved in 1936 to a more spacious site in the nearby Stephansberg district above the cellars where beer from the Schlenkerla was stored.

The young proprietor Matthias Trum, representing the sixth generation of the family to run the company, bubbles over with enthusiasm for the traditions he proudly maintains. It is the only remaining Bamberg brewery to use 100% smoked malt. Matthias led the way to the kiln where his malted barley is gently roasted. Beech-wood logs cut from the surrounding forests are stored alongside the kiln. He opened the door of the kiln, disclosing a red, roaring blaze within. He added some fresh logs to maintain the correct temperature. He uses locally grown barley malt and Hallertauer hops from the fields near Munich. The floral, piny and herbal aromas and flavours of the hops balance the extreme smokiness of the malt, he says.

In common with the Nuremberg brewery, Heller-Trum is based on two simple vessels, a mash kettle and a lauter. The mash of grain and pure hot water is transferred for filtration to the lauter and the clear wort then returns to the first vessel, where it is vigorously boiled with hops. The hopped wort is fermented for a week and is then transferred to the lager cellars beneath the brewery. Matthias took me down steep and perilous stairs to the cool cellars beneath the brewery. He has 14 small lager tanks where the 5.1% *Aecht* (Original) Schlenkerla Rauchbier is matured for two months. *Märzen* (March) and strong Bock beers are also produced and are lagered for three months.

One of the many misconceptions about lager beer is that cold fermentation and storage before the 19th century were purely empirical practices. Brewers stored beer in cellars and noticed that secondary fermentation was slow and free from infection but made no effort to understand why this should be so. Bamberg's history proves this to be wrong.

Lagering was a defined system. Like Rome, the city is built on seven hills and the sandstone cellars were ideal places to store beer. Matthias Trum told me that for centuries ice was cut from the local Regnitz river and packed above the lager cellars. As Bamberg grew in importance and beer volumes increased, local ice was supplemented by ice brought by boats from Finland. Today the cellars at Heller-Trum are kept cool by air conditioning. Carl von Linde, the inventor of refrigeration, came from Franconia and was given financial support by the Bamberg brewers.

The oldest Rauchbier brewery in Bamberg is the Christian Merz Spezial brewpub on Obere Köningstraße. It was founded in 1536 and originally lagered its beer in caves cut from the sandstone on the Stephansberg hill. Visitors can see the entrance to the cave, which is now the serving area for its large beer garden, the Spezial-Keller, on Oberer Stephansberg. History is all around. The long haul up the Michaelsberg hill brings you to the monastery where the former monks' lager cellars house the brewing museum. There is a vast range of old brewing implements and artefacts while a video traces the history of brewing in Franconia.

Bamberg, Freising and Nuremberg provide living proof that lager beer has a history far older than the industrial revolution and the 19th century. It stands alongside ale as part of the rich tapestry of brewing down the ages. It demands greater appreciation from drinkers and more care and attention from some modern producers of the style.

CHAPTER ELEVEN

ALE-WYFES & BEER-CHEFS
THE EVOLUTION OF COOKING WITH BEER

Lucy Saunders

Archaeological records from about 8000BC prove the existence of fermentation. In fact, the most ancient recipe yet discovered is a collection of Sumerian stone tablets engraved with methods to bake bread and use the loaves to ferment a drink 'which makes anyone who tastes it feel blissful and exhilarated.' Ahhh, beer.

By the time the Domesday Book was compiled in England in 1086AD, brewing was an established part of domestic life across settlements in the northern hemisphere, as well as parts of South America and middle Asia. As a safe alternative to water from polluted rivers, wells or cisterns, beer added flavour and nutrition. It was a dietary staple, so cooking with beer was convenient – as often the household's cook did the brewing, too. In England, this is how the moniker *alewyfe*, came to be.[1]

The Tudor era in England was when a quart of ale was renowned as 'a dish fit for a king' in Shakespeare's *Winter's Tale*. The era seems a fitting start for this essay, a high point from which to explore a few of the first printed recipes for cooking with beer, and follow them to learn about the global traditions behind the recipes. Historic records of domestic and monastic beer cookery meander through the text, and then modern professional beer-chefs shall have their say. (My restriction is fluency only in English and French, so some key recipes in other languages may be omitted.)

What recipes are available for cooking with beer? Documented recipes naturally follow education, literacy, and the growth of printing. By the 16th century, cookbooks for the

English gentry had reached the wealthy middle classes, inspiring culinary creativity.

> Take Ale and set it on the fire, and when it seetheth
> scum it, and then put in your Sparrowes and small
> Raisins, Sugar and Sinamon, Ginger and Date, and let
> them boyle together, and then take marrows or Butter,
> and a little Vergiuos, and keepe it close. And when it is
> enough, make sops in platters and serve them forth.
>
> *A Book of Cookrye,* AW, 1591[2]

About five percent of the recipes catalogued for *Cooking with Shakespeare* use ale in some form, according to co-author Mark Morton. 'It was common to cook with beer as it was easy to get,' says Morton. 'In Queen Elizabeth's court, everyone was allotted a gallon and a half of small beer per day.'

The low gravity ales of about 2.5% alcohol by volume were often brewed with spices most complementary to cooking: sweet gale, coriander, fennel, or the more costly ginger, cloves, and grains of paradise, imported from Asia.

During 'Tudor Cookery Days' at the Bayleaf Farmhouse at Winkworth Farm, part of the Weald and Downland Open Air Museum at Singleton, Chichester, the cook prepared pies, joints of meat, and home-brewed ales.[3]

> Take a legge of mutton and cutte it in small slices and
> put it in a chafter and put thereto a pottell of ale, and
> scome it clene, then put thereto seven or eighte onions
> thin sliced and after thei have boylde one houre put
> therto a disshe of swete butter and so let theim boyle till
> thei be tender and then put therto a litle peper and salte.
>
> *A Propre New Booke of Cokery,* Anon., 1545

Food and beer found their places at tables high and low. Ale and beer were essential foodstuffs, consumed as liquid nourishments by persons of all ages and classes and used in both cooking and healing.[4] In a 16th-century ledger from the estate of the Duke of

Clarence in Northumberland records show that the high consumption of beer for the household of almost 300 people (more than half of them servants) made it an economic necessity to brew on site.[5] Some exceptions existed, mostly for royal households close by monastery breweries.

The monastic brewing tradition set beer's place at those tables, even if served as 'liquid bread.' Ale was often used to cook eggs, as in possets and the 14th-century recipe for 'caudles.'[6] Sops,[7] possets[8] and soups made with beer and cream also appear. Melted cheese mixed with ale and served over toasted bread was a staple dish called a Welsh rarebit, or Welsh rabbit.

Another iconic combination, the beer cheese soup, might have descended from the beer and heavy cream soups favoured in Scandinavia and Denmark. (This might account for the popularity of beer and cheese soup in northern regions of the USA which were largely settled by immigrants from these countries. Wisconsin beer cheese soup is a perfect pairing of two of the state's top agricultural products.)

Belgian monasteries are famous for innovations in beer and brewing, and sometimes used beer as an ingredient, mostly rind-washed cheeses made with ale. Belgian monasteries began brewing in the early 10th century, but the restricted diets of monastic life served food as simply prepared as possible, in order not to incite any overly carnal desires!

Fritters, batters, and even waffles made with beer are listed in early Belgian and English cookery texts. Here is a 16th-century recipe for sweet and savory spinach fritters from *The Good Huswife's Jewell* of 1596 by Thomas Dawson:

Take a good deal of Spinnedge, and washe it cleane,
then boyle it in faire water, and when it is boyled, then
take it forth and let the water runne from it, then chop
it with the backe of a knife, and then put in some egges
and grated Bread and season it with suger, sinamon,
ginger and pepper, dates minced fine, and currans, and
rowle them like a ball and dippe them in a Batter made
of Ale and flower, to fry.

In Scandinavia, beer was used to pickle fish, make batters, and blended with molasses and ginger to make a savoury gingerbread. Northern Europeans also experimented with wassails and Christmas ales, baked with spiced dried fruits to make winter compotes.

German cooking with beer follows the trend. The Abbey at St Gallen had several breweries in operation by the 9th century. By the 15th century, German beers included standard brown ales as well as weiss biers, which were served at breakfast, alongside one of the more than 1,500 regional variations of sausage, presented with sweet mustard, butter, and bread or rolls. Sometimes, potato pancakes were prepared with beer in the batter, which was thought to keep the cakes from sticking to the skillet. Diners could choose from pork, boar or lamb roasts glazed with beer, as in the Franconian *schäuferle*, chicken cooked in beer and onions, as well as pickled salads, dense granary breads, bier dumplings, and marinades for roasted meats, chicken, and fish.

Vegetables of all kinds could be prepared with ale. An early 16th-century English recipe for Boiled Sallet (salad) made with Burrage (borage), Endiffe (endive), Coleflower (cauliflower), Sorrel, Marigold, Watercresses, Sparragus (asparagus), Rocket (arugula), garnished with hardboiled eggs, was dressed with ale and mustard.

Most importantly, beer was a preferred drink for travel, as living ales in casks could keep safely on long sea voyages without turning into vinegar. Beer was a beverage to sustain pilgrims such as Martin Luther, and by the 16th century, the German Einbeck, a strong bockbier was shipped as far away as Jerusalem.[9]

Cask ale was one of the staples for explorers, sailors and buccaneers, with beer used to moisten rations such as dried fish and pickled vegetables into a chopped *sallad-magundy*.[10] But beer and brewing was already established in at least one 'newly discovered' continent – South America.

In Mesoamerica, amaranth was cultivated about 5,500 years ago and used to make a fermented drink akin to beer. Aztec ruins from 3,100 years ago point to the preparation of fermented cocoa ale, made from cacoa beans. A fermented beer of agaves and maize was served at Mayan religious ceremonies. The maize beer called *chicha* is indigenous to Ecuador; its origins dating to circa 1000BC.

Brewing *chicha* was a big business for women in Latin America. By the 19th century, Bolivian *chicharias* became an entire female cottage industry monopoly. Variations on chicha are found throughout the continent now, along with lager brews introduced in the last 100 years. Latin cooks use beer to braise roasted meats, marinate beef, vegetables and chicken, and in preparing slow-cooked beans, as in *frijoles borrachos* (drunken beans).[11]

Beer cookery went with the immigrants to North America. Colonial cooks made beer brewed from foodstuffs from persimmons to pumpkins, and used the ales to make fritters, soups and braised meats. Several varieties of johnnycakes, or cornbread baked in a skillet, used beer. Native Americans used sap extracted from sugar maple trees to make a fermented hominy drink, and from them, New Englanders learned to make maple beer.

Recipe collections and cookery books gained in popularity as a means to civilise natives and teach literacy through the universal language of food. Beer and brewing arts were most valued. Early American villages maintained community cookbooks, which would be updated as recipes were used and adapted. A recipe collection for community use by Anne Lisle from 1748 includes an 'ale recipe from which my mother Mrs Lisle brews eight hogsheads.'[12] Ales were used to make vinegars and mustards, as well as dozens of cakes, breads, cheeses, sauces, and even a strong ale tomato ketchup touted to keep for at least 20 years!

By the 19th century, most beer cookery was still limited to home kitchens, with the exception of beer-batter fish and chips stands and the occasional *carbonnades* served in authentic restaurants. In America, the effects of Prohibition, global warfare, mass migrations, and commercial standardisation of light lagers meant that by the mid-20th century, beer cuisine was becoming a family secret.

After Prohibition, many American breweries released brand-name beer cookbooks or recipe pamphlets for promotional purposes. This public relations effort presented a typical array of foods prepared with beer, but each recipe bore the name of the brand – a dulling exercise in repetitive marketing. Worse yet, traditional Belgian beer recipes were plundered for public relations to promote cooking with sodas and colas during the 1950s and 1960s, explaining the origins of recipes such as chicken braised in root beer.

Some influential food critics in the USA resisted the relentless placement of brand names in beer recipes. For example, the *New York Times* food writer Craig Claiborne was fairly dismissive in this snippet from 1984:

> Beer is one of the world's most favourite drinks, and most Americans think of it as just that and nothing more. Curious, because it is by no means a novelty in cooking. In the world of international cuisine, perhaps the best known of all beer dishes is the carbonade flamande of Belgium, a dish made with cubed beef, a lot of onions and a conspicuous quantity of light beer. Books have been written on cooking with beer ... it is not at all surprising to find it used in recipes that call for a leavening agent. We are not all that enthusiastic about the universal use of beer in the kitchen with one exception, and that is as a beer batter. A batter containing beer as a leavening agent is perhaps the finest of all. It is also one of the easiest of deep-frying batters to prepare, as it has a multitude of application.[13]

Beer cuisine seemed to be stuck with stews and fritters. Perhaps that made sense, because in 1984, much of North America was stuck with mass-market Pilsners. Then craft brewing came along, and changed the contents of beer coolers and retailers: from stouts, to Belgian *dubbels*, to cherry-laced wood-aged *saisons*, there are now more than 175 styles of beer available in the USA.

Today's beer-chefs find inspiration in the old ways, seeking out the recipes of grandmothers and great grandmothers. Modern chefs are bringing beer as an ingredient into the kitchens of restaurants, bistros, taverns, brewpubs, gastro pubs, and cafés. The culinary exploration mirrors the explosion in beer styles thanks to modern craft brewers.

With the wave comes growing interest in historic beer cuisine, such as chicken cooked in cream and ale, to lamb shanks braised in beer with shallots, herbs and heirloom fingerling potatoes. Sometimes, old family recipes for cooking with beer take only a bit of tweaking to modernise.

For example, *Poulet à la Blanche du Chambly* from Quebec chef Francois Pellerin was featured at the SAVOR festival in Washington DC in May 2008. Its base, a creamy beurre blanc sauce to dress the cooked chicken, was prepared with some witbier, spiced with coriander just as a 16th-century ale would be.

This trend echoes the rediscovery of other old-fashioned culinary techniques such as brining and home-curing meats, preserving and pickling, which some of the best beer-chefs also practice. Greg Higgins of Portland, Oregon's Higgins Tavern, prepares many of the pickles, relishes, and cured meats in-house for signature flavour, sometimes incorporating beer into the process.

No less a celebrated cuisinier than Stefaan Couttenye of Watou, Belgium, acknowledges his debts to his grandmothers and family. 'Cooking with beer is a family tradition,' he says in his book, *Cooking with Beer at 't Hommelhof* co-authored by Jon Van Hemeledonck (Roularta Books, 1999).

Most of all, cooking with beer is popular in Belgium both in restaurants and family kitchens, perhaps as a result of the stunning variety of beer styles brewed in the country and a national appreciation of gastronomy.

Even the ubiquitous Belgian *moules frites*, a hot pot of mussels steamed in ale and served with crisp-fried potatoes accompanied by *aioli* or garlic mayonnaise, can be found prepared with dozens of different ales and lambics.

Jean Rodriguez, of the In't Spinnekopke in Brussels, is one of

Belgium's leading beer-chefs and an inspiration to many beer aficionados. His cookbook, *Cuisine Facile à la Bière*, is one of the best references for family-style cooking with beer, including eel steamed in lambic with shallots, lemon and parsley, a house speciality, or salmon poached in witbier sauce.[14]

As many chefs visit Belgium and discover their fantastic brewing traditions, they learn to appreciate beer's place at the table, and in the kitchen. Chef Eric Lehousse of Montreal's Le Petit Moulinsart lived in Belgium for a decade, working in his grandmother's restaurant. Lehousse said in an interview with Raymond Beauchemin, 'I learned a lot about *cuisine de terroire*, what my grandmother used to do, and she learned it from her grandmother – these are not the traditions that you learn about in culinary school.'[15]

Lehousse's experience is typical, as travel for apprenticeships, cookbooks and experimentation continue to be the mainstays of teaching beer cuisine. Just one professional culinary school in the US, Johnson & Wales, offers students an education in craft beer appreciation, and that is centred on their campus in Denver, one of the USA's leading cities for breweries and brewpubs.

I could not find any examples of professional culinary programs in the UK or Europe that regularly include beer appreciation and beer cookery in the classroom curriculum. However, several chefs conduct classes and tastings in their restaurants or pub kitchens. The Campaign for Real Ale supports cooking with beer through recipes printed in newsletters, cookbooks, and culinary beer appreciation guides such as Fiona and Will Beckett's *An Appetite for Ale* (CAMRA, 2007).

Extra-curricular clubs and festivals for beer appreciation are the most frequent resources to help student chefs learn about beer flavours. The Great American Beer Festival™, held in Denver each October, now offers several short cooking and food-pairing demonstrations on each day of the festival. Local culinary students can gain experience by assisting at the demonstrations, featuring top American beer-chefs such as Bruce Paton of San Francisco's Cathedral Hotel.

Yet much more remains to be discovered. In many ways,

people who consider themselves to be 'gourmets' just don't respect beer. A diner once told me this rule of thumb in his beverage selection, 'If I can eat it with my hands in a restaurant, then I'll choose a beer. So, burgers and skewers and hotdogs are the foods I'll have with beer. But if I'm using cutlery, then I'll choose wine.' He was quite smug about this tyrannical rule of the opposable thumb – hand-held foods with beer, fork-lifted foods with wine. He couldn't imagine how a beer's flavour, aromatics and texture might actually make it the superior choice for the table setting.

Even more people associate beer with slaking thirst alone, and will only drink beer when it's hot outside, and the beer is ice-cold. 'I only drink beer during the summer and then only with typical cook-out foods, such as burgers and ribs,' another woman told me.

Such prejudices might be erased with more guidance from restaurant chefs and servers, more tastings, and inspiring choices in beer cuisine.

There are a few pioneers for better beer and food together at the table; two of the early adopters were Charles and Rose Anne Finkel of the Pike Pub & Brewery in Seattle. Their tastings and events bring together groups such as Les Dames d'Escoffier in the appreciation of beer and food. Pike's chef Richard Marx favours local foodstuffs, prepared with their beers and sometimes even brewing ingredients, as in chocolate truffles spiked with Imperial Stout and rolled in crushed black barley malt.

One of the reasons I champion beer as an ingredient is presenting the bridge that will naturally connect the flavours of the dish with the diner and the drink. And it's why I respect the mission of the Canadian restaurant named beerbistro, which is 'to change the way people think about beer.'

Chef-owner Brian Morin is one of Toronto's leading chefs for *cuisine à la biere*, and co-author of an upcoming beerbistro cookbook with Canadian beer authority, Stephen Beaumont. 'I think of a beer as a set of flavours to explore,' Morin says. 'The obvious starting point is with a beer's history and place because there are regional influences in cuisine.'

'Beer is still a really undiscovered ingredient for so many cooks,' says Morin. 'Perhaps that's because chefs need to adapt cooking techniques to keep the flavours of beer fresh and appealing.' Morin often uses beer as a finishing touch to sauces, avoiding the intense heat the might render an ale too bitter. The moderate acidity of beer makes it an excellent foil to the mineral flavours in vegetables, such as the beerbistro's pasta stuffed with spinach, shallots, garlic, black truffles and a broth of Belgian ale and grated Parmesan, served with a somewhat spicy *saison* ale.

For many chefs, supporting local breweries means understanding local beer styles. Sue Nowak, British food writer and author of many pub guides for CAMRA, has championed authentic English styles, such as cask-conditioned mild ales. In addition to three cookbooks, Nowak creates style-specific recipes to prove how food-friendly beer can be.

Home-brewing is another avenue to the art of cooking with beer. Californian Sean Paxton brings a chef's sensibilities to making beer, and also experiments with beer cuisine through catering festivals and home-brew competitions. His advice in cooking with beer is to taste, and taste widely, to discern the elements of raw foods and spices – such plum, pine, or peppercorns – in a beer. He lets those tastes and aromatics guide him to find the right recipe, one that will complement or highlight those flavours.

Chicago-based Randy Mosher is an author and expert in home-brewing exotic ales with food ingredients such as flavourful tinctures of chanterelle mushrooms soaked in spirits. He often experiments with cooking with beer and pairings. Mosher says, 'How is it that wine, the beverage that claims primacy at the table, can completely write off soup and salad courses, spicy cuisine and most vegetables, is weak-kneed in the presence of cheese, and can only feebly whisper 'port' when the subject of chocolate comes up ... clearly, there are cracks in the castle walls. Time to storm the gates.'[16]

It's a beer revolution, or better still, a revelation. Beer can be part of the professional chef's pantry, as well as part of a secret family recipe from an ancestral alewyfe.

How to make an ale piecrust, based on the following 1594 recipe:

Take Butter and Ale and seeth them together: then take your flower and put therinto three Egs, Sugar, Saffron and salt.

The modern version:
½ cup butter
¼ cup brown ale
1½ cups white flour
2 large eggs
2 tablespoons turbinado sugar
6 threads saffron
½ teaspoon salt
Bring ale and butter to a low boil in a small saucepan, stirring, until butter melts. Let cool to lukewarm, and beat in eggs. When emulsified, add remaining ingredients, working into flour until dough is of a uniform consistency. Scrape onto a floured surface and roll out. Makes a double nine-inch crust.

Adapted by Mark Morton for *Cooking with Shakespeare.*

NOTES

1   In Scotland she was known as *yill-wife.*
2   Morton, Mark and Coppolino, Andrew. *Cooking with Shakespeare.* Westport, CT, Greenwood Press, 2008.
3   Tait, Simon. *Feasting on a taste of history.* Freelance article. London.
4   Bennett, Judith M. *Ale, Beer, and Brewsters in England: Women's Work in a Changing World.* New York: Oxford University Press, 1996.
5   Van Brunt Jones, Paul. *The Household of a Tudor Nobleman.* Torch Press, 1918.
6   A warm drink made from wine or ale mixed with sugar, eggs, bread and spices.
7   According to Chambers: a piece of food, especially bread, dipped or soaked in a liquid, eg soup.
8   According to Chambers: a drink of hot milk, curdled with wine, ale or vinegar, and flavoured with spices, formerly used as a remedy for colds, etc.

9 Winship, Kihm. *The Beers of Martin Luther.* EnjoyingBeer.com, 2007.

10 Wilk, Richard and Hintlian, P. *Cooking on their own: Cuisines of manly men.* Food & Foodways, 13:159-168, 2005.

11 Kiple, Kenneth F. *A Movable Feast: Ten Millennia of Food Globalization.* Cambridge University Press, 2007.

12 Sherman, Sandra. *The Whole Art and Mystery of Cooking: What Cookbooks Taught Readers in the Eighteenth Century.* Journal of Eighteenth Century Life, Volume 28, No. 1, 2004.

13 Claiborne, Craig, and Franey, Pierre. *Beer Rises to the Occasion. New York Times,* 3 June, 1984 (p. SM 92).

14 Herman, Paul and Rodriguez, Jean. *Cuisine Facile à la Bière* (illustrations de Godi). Glénat Benelux, Bruxelles, 1989.

15 Beauchemin, Raymond. *Beer Secrets: interview with Chef Eric Lehousse. The Montreal Gazette,* 25 August 2002.

16 Mosher, Randy. From the Preface in *Best of American Beer & Food* by Saunders, Lucy. Brewers Publications, Denver, 2007.

CHAPTER TWELVE
IN SEARCH OF GERMAN BEER CULTURE

Conrad Seidl

To get a picture of Germany's beer culture it may be a good approach to look at it from the outside, for example at a visit to the GermanFest. This festival is held annually in Milwaukee, a town famous for its rich tradition in brewing. In the 19th century brewers from Germany began to settle down on the shores of Lake Michigan and built breweries. Their names, August Krug, Frederic Miller, Johann Braun, Valentine Blatz, Gottlieb Heileman(n) and Frederick Pabst, all indicated the German origin of the breweries – and Joseph Schlitz, a bookkeeper from the German town of Mainz, started his own brewing business in 1858 by acquiring August Krug's brewery. Thirteen years later his marketing claim 'the beer that made Milwaukee famous' would continue to work for many decades. The brewers' names alone signalled high beer quality.

Milwaukee must have been a beer drinker's paradise in the days of Schlitz and Pabst, Blatz and Miller. It had all the elements that constitute a robust beer culture, namely several competing breweries with a broad portfolio of different beers, offered in style to knowledgeable consumers. Very little of that tradition can be found on a visit to a GermanFest today. There are thousands of visitors in something akin to traditional national costume who come to listen to mainstream folk music played by bands from Germany and Austria, eat what is called 'German Pizza' (a dish unknown in Germany) and drink lots of Miller Lite from the last large brewery operating in town.

Of course every German visitor who attends this American

festival would laugh at this caricature of German beer culture –
and so would any serious beer drinker: does this festival have
anything to do with what we believe to be true German beer
culture? Germans would talk about the 1300 breweries in their
country, the tradition of beer gardens and beer halls in Bavaria
and the 160 breweries in neighbouring Austria. And most of all
they would recommend visiting the Oktoberfest in Munich to get
a 'real' picture of Germany's beer culture.

Well, let's have a closer look at this. Is it really that different?
We can find thousands of festival-goers at the Oktoberfest who
pour into the big tents to listen to mainstream folk music
performed by bands from Germany (and in recent years more
often from Austria and the Czech Republic), eat pork knuckles
and drink lots of Oktoberfest beer, most of which is brewed by
the giants Inbev (Löwenbräu, Spaten) and Heineken (Paulaner,
Hacker-Pschorr). Okay, there is a little difference: there is no beer
brewed by SAB Miller at the Oktoberfest but there are beers from
smaller local breweries too – Sprecher in the case of Milwaukee
and Augustiner and Hofbräuhaus at Munich's Oktoberfest.

The similarities are striking: German beer culture is perceived
as excessive consumption of mainstream beer to the *mhpftata*-
sound of brass bands. There is some truth to that myth – at least
during the 16 days of the Oktoberfest which oddly takes place in
September. It must be tempting for any entrepreneur in the beer
business anywhere in the world to mimic the Oktoberfest or the
vast beer halls of Munich's Hofbräuhaus which, for most of the
time, are populated by large crowds of tourists who get what they
are expecting, so most German beer bars anywhere in the world
try to replicate precisely that atmosphere.

This concept is so popular that it even works in most large
German towns: many of them feature at least one 'Bavarian Style'
beer bar – after all, people from other regions of Germany visit
Munich as tourists from time to time. Bavarian bars in their
hometown would seem authentic even to them.

Don't they have their own beer culture? Oh yes, they have. In
most regions of Germany you may find a rich brewing tradition
or at least traces of that tradition. But in the last 150 years or so

Munich's interpretation of beer and beer culture has dominated the perception of what is 'real' beer culture. In the 19th century it would guarantee choice and style, quality and authenticity. Very little of this has survived.

On the other hand, most German beer drinkers don't care. Their drink of choice is a pale lager – invariably referred to as *Pils* although many of these beers lack the bitterness that is characteristic for the style. German beer statistics record about two thirds of overall beer production as Pilsners – which includes beers as full bodied as Berliner Bürgerbräu's Bio-Pils, as bitter as Jever, as aromatic as Waldhaus and as soft as Warsteiner. It also includes Oettinger, which is probably Germany's least respected brand with a non-existent marketing budget; it is the bestselling brand simply because it is heavily discounted. On this basis, it may be worthwhile to look again at our attempt to trace German beer culture. Oettinger's success takes you hundreds of miles from Munich into the forests in Franconia.

This is where Günther Kollmar was born, the man who has revolutionised the German beer business in the last two decades. The village of Fürnheim looks as if it has been untouched for much longer: most of the roads in the area are unpaved; the church is the dominant structure amidst two dozen small farmhouse-like buildings and there is a curious sign that states, 'The brewery is right across the street from the church.' It is.

The Forstquell Brewery is a brewpub that was built into the former brewery building of the Kollmar family who acquired the brewery in nearby Oettingen in 1956. Oettinger has grown to be Germany's largest beer brand with an annual production of 6.73m hectolitres produced in five breweries across the republic – but Kollmar acts as if the sixth brewery, the one in Fürnheim, is the most important. This small brewery brews the most traditional beers in the group, including Forstquell Kupfer, an amber-coloured beer with a flowery nose reminiscent of roses and a hearty, full-bodied mouth feel. It is easy to imagine how local beers had a similar character for many decades, possibly centuries, although many must have been a lot more hoppy than this one.

But would people drink hoppier beers? Haven't they learned

to prefer bland mainstream lagers? Yes, they have. But having been a brewer for the better part of his life, at the age of 72 Kollmar goes for taste and aroma. At a tasting of his Oettinger Pils he ponders if this beer should be at least a little bit hoppier to meet the expectations of a beer connoisseur. Then again he has to mass-market his brews and the average German consumer believes that German beers are the best in the world, but his tasting experience is very limited. Beers with a distinctive taste are hard to sell to people who are used to drinking mainstream lagers and who consider a Hefeweizen to be a very exotic choice.

Hefeweizen used to be a local beer style in southern Bavaria up to the 1960s and was on the point of disappearing when pale lagers became the drink of choice. It was popular with older consumers – notably women – and Werner Brombach, owner of the now famous Erdinger Weissbräu near Munich, feared that demand would be down to zero by 1990 when his loyal customers were expected to have passed away. So he decided to reposition his product to appeal to a much younger crowd – weissbier became a lifestyle drink that was closely associated with Bavaria, tourism and the beer gardens that play a much more important role in southern Germany than in other parts of the country.

The success of Hefeweizen not only helped Erdinger to become one of the leading privately owned breweries in Germany, it also encouraged other breweries to venture into the speciality beer market. So far this success has been unparalleled and has actually overshadowed the decline of other local beer styles from Alt to Berliner Weisse.

These local styles have been highly respected for centuries. In 1575 Heinrich Knaust wrote one of the earliest books on German beer. He listed 133 local beer styles, virtually all of which are now extinct; now there is no Benichen beer in Lüneburg, no Schluntz in Erfurt and no trace of a beer style named Israel in Lübeck. Knaust, who was not only a seasoned traveller but also a philosopher, described Israel as a wheat beer that was so strong that the drinker's body had to wrestle with it as Jacob had done with the angel!

One other aspect in Knaust's record is of interest: while he focused on Germany he also included several places that did not sound German today, but have been part of German Reich for centuries. Prague (Prag in German, Praha in Czech), for example, had a significant German-speaking population until 1945, as had Danzig (Gdansk in Poland), Grätz (Grodzisk Wielkopolski), Straßburg (Strasbourg in France), Pilsen (Plzen in the Czech Republic) and Budweis (Ceske Budejovice). All these places had their own local beers that were once considered to be part of the German brewing heritage.

For centuries it was not Bavaria but rather Bohemia that was famous for wheat beers. We know very little about the brewing recipes but we know that beers were hoppier – and that they travelled well. Albrecht Wenzel Wallenstein, a warlord in the Thirty Years War used to secure a supply of Bohemian wheat beers for himself and his officers when he campaigned in areas like Stralsund (1627), Lübeck (1629), Nürnberg (1632) and Leipzig (1632). All these towns were famous for their local beers – but Bohemian beers were considered superior to them.

It was German brewers who secured the fame of Bohemian beer: for the urban (German-speaking) population and their municipal governments, the crafts of brewing and malting were among the most cherished, having been granted successively by several Bohemian monarchs. The earliest such privileges date back to 1070, and Duke Subieslas II confirmed these with the remark: 'that the Germans who differ in their natures from the Czechs, should also be divided from them in their laws and customs, and that they must be allowed to live according to the laws and judicial practices of the Germans, to all of which they had been accustomed ever since the days of King Wratislas.'

But these privileges were revoked during and after the religious wars of the 16th and 17th centuries: After the peace accord of 1517, the towns had their brewing privileges confined to within the town walls, and the right to establish a 'Bannmeile' (an area up to seven kilometres from the town in which only beer brewed within the town could be sold) was taken from them.

Wherever noblemen (who were more loyal to the king and the church) established breweries and taverns in the rural districts, these proved to be more commercially successful. Brewing rapidly developed in rural Bohemia – and it was extremely profitable: peasants had to deliver crops and cheap labour to their masters and the only beer they could buy was what their masters brewed. Many of today's famous breweries – like Krusovice, founded in 1581 – date from this era.

After the Protestant nobility (who were allied with Protestant burghers in Bohemian towns) was defeated in the Battle on the White Hill on 8 November 1620, breweries worth up to 20 million guilders were confiscated and handed over to Catholic noblemen loyal to the Hapsburg family. It took the Bohemian towns, their Czech-speaking population and their brewers almost three centuries to recover from that defeat. Even the now famous Pilsner Brewery (Plzensky Prazdoj) went into operation in 1842 as a purely German company named Bürgerliches Brauhaus, run by a Bavarian head brewer named Joseph Groll who is credited with inventing the first Pilsner-style beer.

Shortly afterwards drinking beer – drinking the right beer – became a political issue. Several Czech breweries were created for political reasons in the second half of the 19th century: nationalist investors founded these companies (Prague's Staropramen in 1871 and Budweis' Budvar in 1895) so that Czech people would not have to drink beer brewed by German brewers. These 19th-century concerns brewed modern bottom-fermenting lager beers like Pilsner Urquell and dark lagers that were typical of Munich and Prague in the late 19th century. Unfortunately we have little knowledge about the top-fermenting beers that were the standard drink in most parts of central Europe before the industrial-scale production of lagers started in Pilsen, Munich, Dortmund and Vienna around the middle of the 19th century. But it is safe to assume that these ales were generally hoppier than what we drink nowadays – hops were the most powerful agent at keeping bacterial infections under control and the beer as fresh as possible.

Considering the low standards of hygiene at that time it may be safe to assume that even Hefeweizen beers were heavily hopped to make them as stable as possible. These top-fermenting beers were especially prone to lactic infections that could be efficiently suppressed by a high dosage of alpha acids. We will never know for certain (as brewing recipes tend to be unspecific and analysis of brewing materials of former times is unavailable) but the Weizenbier that Wallenstein had delivered to his military camp may very well have been as hoppy as today's Schneider Wiesen Edelweisse or even the Schneider-Brooklyner Hopfen-Weisse – two wheat beers that are so distinctive in taste and aroma that the Schneider Brewery makes them only for export to the US because even seasoned German drinkers of Hefeweizen would hardly appreciate their unique character.

Let us take the speculation one step further: what would a 17th-century military commander expect from a beer that was shipped across several borders to his headquarters? Of course this beer must have been too expensive to be the regular drink for Wallenstein's troops. An army of 20,000 to 35,000 men could not be supplied with a beer that had to be transported for several weeks. But this beer may have been a delicacy to those who knew how to enjoy it – even during the time of Europe's most devastating war.[1]

It may sound surprising but beer was an important and valuable commodity four or five centuries ago – it could not be mass-produced then and the limited supply made it even more valuable. It was not uncommon for noblemen to send casks of a special brew from their local brewery as a special gift to a king. Some breweries even specialised in the production of beers that would transport well and survive the month-long journey on horse-drawn carriages.

High levels of hops, a high alcohol content and, in many cases, a higher acidity than we would find tolerable today, helped preserve those beers – Einbeck's first bock-style beers must have had all these virtues. It is surprising that hardly any of the brewpubs and microbreweries in Germany have tried to recreate such beers as these.

German brew masters tend to assume that beers have always been more or less similar to those that they brew today. Even when challenged to brew an example of an historic beer they will try to stay on the safe side and make it as close as possible to what they are used to brewing. But of course there are rare and noteworthy exceptions to this rule. In Plaue, about 30 kilometres west of Berlin, there is a small brewpub called Kneipe Pur, where Gernot Brätz brews beers far beyond the Reinheitsgebot (the so called 'purity law' that limits the ingredients of beer to water, malted barley and hops) – he has ventured into brewing a 'German Stout,' an ale containing stinging nettles and even a 'Garlic Beer.' One of the beer styles Brätz tried to re-invent is the Kirsch-Mumme, a fruit beer that was popular in Braunschweig up to the 18th century.

Mumme is another good example of a beer that was widely exported for some time – in this case between circa 1500 and 1730 – but went out of fashion. There were at least three qualities of this dark ale: a strong version for export (the so-called Schiffs-mumme as it was transported on ships to England), a somewhat lighter Stadtmumme for everyday consumption in the town of Braunschweig and the previously mentioned Kirsch-Mumme that underwent a secondary fermentation when cherries were added. There is only one of the historic Mumme breweries left in town – it produces a malt extract they call Mumme and suggest adding this syrup-like brew to a standard lager beer to make it more full-bodied. This late descendant of the traditional brew is more often used as an ingredient in baking.

It would be thrilling to see beers like this re-created just as various versions of porters, stouts and pale ales have been reborn in small craft breweries in the US. But there is no similar craft brewing movement in Germany. There are 600 brewpubs (called Gasthausbrauerei in German) – but only a handful of them dare to brew unique beers. The standard beer in a Gasthausbrauerei will be an unfiltered lager and the brewer will try to optimise its drinkability to a point where it can hardly be distinguished from an industrial product. The same approach will be taken to the production of that brewpub's Hefeweizen. All marketing will focus on the freshness of the brews rather than on taste and the customers will learn very little about the choice a brewpub could offer.

Another fine example of a brewpub off the beaten track can

be found in southern Austria. In Kalsdorf, between Graz and the Styrian hop-growing region in Leutschach, Handbrauerei Forstner is situated. Here Gerhard Forstner brews some of the strongest and most remarkable beers in the German-speaking world – including a herbal brew called Wunder-bier. Brewing beer using absinthe and other spices is easier in Austria because the Reinheitsgebot does not apply here and brewers have a choice of ingredients that are banned in Germany.

Some old brewing traditions call for ingredients that are outlawed by the Reinheitsgebot: Leipzig's traditional gose is a wheat beer that under-goes a lactic secondary fermentation. The beer is spiced with coriander and salt which results in a refreshing but very dry overall impression – the salty aftertaste makes the gose drinker even thirstier. It has taken several years for this traditional brewing method to be legalised again in Saxony where there are two breweries making the local speciality beer.

On the other hand there are beers that purport to being brewed to very old recipes but are neither as old nor as traditional as the breweries suggest. The most famous example is the altbier, a style that carries age ('alt' means old) in its name: brewers insist that the name comes from the old production methods including the use of top-fermenting yeast and the practice of dry hopping. Undoubtedly there have been beers produced in the past using these methods, but probably not the cold maturation in lager tanks that is practiced today. But did these beers constitute a style of their own? The name altbier seems to appear only after 1945 when people longed for a name that reminded them of the pre-war beers.

Even if altbiers are not as old as their name suggests, visiting an altbier brewery in downtown Düsseldorf may be one of the better ways to experience genuine German beer culture. The brewery taps of Uerige, Füchschen, Schlüssel and Schumacher offer an authentic atmosphere as well as a beer that differs enormously from the standard offer in other beer bars – in that respect Düsseldorf's bars are more interesting than those in its rival Cologne that offer the local Kölsch beer. Kölsch is much closer to the ubiquitous Pilsners than altbier which is generally dark, aromatic with some nutty notes and, of course, a lot hoppier. Kölsch beers on the other hand have been dumbed down in the course of the last four decades: records from the late 1950s and early 1960s show that the Kölsch beers of the time were on the bitter side, being even spicier in their hop flavour than the Pilsners.

But authentic beer culture is about being different from the mainstream. This sort of beer culture can be found in Germany – but you have to know where to look. Take Jena for example: this university town in Thuringia used to be as famous for its tart and acidic weisse as Berlin. Berliner weisse in its pure form is hard to find these days (if it is found at all it will be served – sometimes even pre-mixed – with raspberry or woodruff syrup which destroys the delicate aroma).

Jenaer weisse is an even more obscure beer style and most inhabitants of Jena would have no idea that it even survived World War II and four decades of Communist rule. Yet a small brewpub on the outskirts of Jena, the Talschänke, brews this gemstone of German brewing tradition. Do not expect too much from the pub – in fact it is one of the least attractive in town and it is no match for the breweries and brewpubs of Düsseldorf and Cologne. But the beer is worth the trip; possibly the best beer to pair with any fish dish.

And once you are there take the chance to plan a trip southward. Along the railway to Nürnberg you will pass some small towns that are home to some of the most unspoilt family breweries in Germany. Even in Bamberg, one of the hotspots of tourism in the region there are brewery taps that offer unique beers. Schlenkerla with its famous smoky Rauchbier (which also comes as a Rauch-Bock and a Rauch-Weizen) may be the most prominent example, but do not ignore Fässla, an unspoilt brewery tap that offers fine examples of the most common south-German beer styles starting with a Bavarian style Helles, a hoppy Pilsner, the local dark Franconian lager, a Doppelbock and two versions of Weizenbier. All this is served in a very traditional atmosphere, a dimly lit tavern with half a dozen tables, no food, but excellent beer served by gravity from wooden casks.

Is this the ultimate place to find German beer culture? Maybe it is. There may be better locations, even more interesting beers. Many will be very close, as Franconia is the region that has the highest density of breweries. Their products are easier to find – and safer to drink – than in the times of warlord Wallenstein who ruled the region in the 17th century.

Just go and try it.

From here you are on your own. But by now you know more about German beer culture than most visitors to the festivals, brewpubs and bars I have mentioned. Have a safe trip. Cheers!

NOTES

1 Twenty-five percent of Germany's population perished in this war.

CHAPTER THIRTEEN
THIRTY YEARS OF
BRITISH BEER

Gavin D Smith

*Before British beer can be enjoyed, experience is required,
but the same could be said for sex. In both cases, mistakes
are inevitably made, but the triumphs make the disasters
worthwhile.*

Michael Jackson

The history of British brewing dates back to pre-Roman times, so
why choose to focus merely on the last three decades? The answer
is twofold.

First, the 1970s saw the beginning of a quiet and rather British
revolution which changed perceptions of beer and brewing, with
the establishment of the Campaign For Real Ale (originally the
Campaign for the Revitalisation of Ale) in 1971. CAMRA now
boasts some 89,000 members and is the most effective British
consumer pressure group of all time, formed with the intention of
challenging what was perceived to be the growing homogenisation of British beer. The movement tapped into concerns
regarding the increasing influence and ubiquity of powerful international corporations and their products, resonating far beyond
the world of beer. The 'small is beautiful' mantra appears to be
deeply embedded in the British public consciousness.
Additionally, a threat to our beer and pubs struck at the very core
of what was considered to be an inviolable aspect of quintessential
British tradition and heritage.

The second reason for isolating the last three decades for

particular study is that six years after the formation of CAMRA, a groundbreaking and highly relevant book was published. Entitled *The World Guide to Beer*, it was written by Michael Jackson, who clearly embraced the essential CAMRA ethos, and almost immediately the volume earned him a place as one of the most influential drinks writers around. He was to confirm that position during the succeeding years with a plethora of important titles on the subjects of beer and subsequently whisky, rapidly outstripping in influence his contemporaries Richard Boston (*Beer and Skittles*) and Michael Dunn (*The Penguin Guide to Real Draught Beer*).

Jackson's *World Guide* was translated into a dozen languages and it was exceptional partly because of its categorisation of beers into stylistic groups within defined geographical parameters. The modern theory of beer 'style' was largely developed by Jackson and expounded in this book, with beer classifications being formalised into the three essential categories of 'bottom-fermented,' 'wheat beers' (also 'bottom-fermented') and 'top-fermented,' with many sub-divisions in each classification.

As Jackson himself wrote, 'Similar books have been written about the beers of individual nations, but such a wide-ranging coverage of the beer-drinking world has not been attempted before.' As well as its categorisation-based approach, one of the factors that made Jackson's study of beer highly unusual at the time was that in his writing he showed a passionate attachment to the locale and the manner in which it was drunk, the food it accompanied, and the heritage of the brewing operations in question.

While countries such as Belgium took a great pride in their beers, the status of beer in Britain during the 1970s was not high. Traditionally, it was seen as a drink of the working classes, and was rarely subject to any form of character-related analysis. By contrast, wine appreciation had long been taken more seriously, and the 1970s saw the emergence of passionate and independent wine advocates and writers such as Robert Parker. With *Beers of the World*, Jackson started the process of becoming to beer what Parker was to wine.

The lack of critical appreciation and evaluation of British beer at the time was not helped by the increasing homogenisation and blandness that CAMRA had been formed to fight against. In truth, there was not too much to appreciate or evaluate.

At the heart of the identity crisis facing British beer was the near-monopoly enjoyed by a handful of large-scale, national brewers. Beer had become dislocated from its regional roots, a state of affairs not helped by the widespread acceptance that unlike wine, or even Scotch malt whisky, there was no such thing as beer *terroir*. Apparently, any brand could be replicated in any location, and as voracious major brewers took over their smaller competitors they used this 'fact' to centralise and rationalise in a manner that was frequently brutal.

Although the process of consolidation reached its apotheosis during the 1960s, it had in fact begun a very long time prior to that decade. In 1840 Britain had boasted no fewer than 50,000 breweries, but just 40 years later that number had halved. In 1900, 6,477 breweries were operating, but by the start of the Second World War in 1939 less than 600 remained, partly due to high levels of taxation and the global recession of the inter-war years.

By the time Jackson penned his *World Guide*, reference was frequently made in brewing circles to the 'Big Six,' which controlled a large percentage of the industry. This sextet comprised Allied Breweries, Bass Charrington, Courage, Scottish & Newcastle, Watney, Mann & Truman and Whitbread. To these Jackson added Guinness and wrote of the 'Big Seven,' who between them boasted a remarkable 91% of the national beer market.

When Jackson's book was published, brewing was no longer just the preserve of traditional brewing companies, either, but also major leisure organisations like Grand Metropolitan Ltd, which since the early 1970s had owned Truman, Hanbury & Buxton Ltd and Watney Mann Ltd. For them, beer and pubs were just part of a much larger commercial picture, and the healthy balance sheets of all the major players in the brewing industry were predicated on the sale of keg beers.

Whereas traditional cask ales are not filtered or processed

after fermentation but racked into casks or bottles as they stand, with secondary fermentation taking place in the cask, 'keg,' canned and most bottled beers are pasteurised to lengthen the beer's life and make it more stable during storage. However, the yeast is killed along with any bacteria, preventing secondary fermentation, and the flavour is therefore often thought to be adversely affected. Keg beers are artificially carbonated to ensure a creamy head at the point of dispensation, while the head on cask ale is a natural part of the brewing process.

Watney, Ind Coope and Whitbread had been the major names behind the widespread promotion of keg beer during the 1960s, which in 1959 accounted for just one percent of total UK beer sales. However, keg beer went on to be used as the principal weapon for major breweries intent on developing national rather than regional powerbases.

The 1960s saw beer sales growing across the board, and 'keg' accounted for 18% of the total by 1971 and 40% by 1976, at which point lager made up more than 20% of the UK beer market. With bottled and canned beers accounting for another 23%, this left 'traditional' cask beer with just 14% of the market.

The attraction of greater profits from economies of scale meant that it was in the big brewers' interests to offer a comparatively small range of products to all their customers, and as keg beer was also more expensive for the consumer than cask beer, usually of lower strength, and kept and travelled well, it is not difficult to see why so much of the brewing industry fell in love with it.

It is important to bear in mind that whilst bemoaning the rise of keg beer, it was popular, in part, because the quality of much of the 'traditional' cask ale on offer was at best variable by the 1970s. Drinkers reasoned that at least with lager or keg beer they got consistency. However, with consistency came ubiquity, and all too often mediocrity, perhaps best embodied by the example of Watney's Red Barrel. Watney's was a brewer with a long and distinguished heritage dating back to 1837, when members of the Watney family took a share in London's Stag Brewery. However, by the 1960s Watney's Red Barrel was the most popular, and highly promoted, keg beer in Britain, though in terms of actual character there was little to differentiate it from many of its rivals.

Such was its perceived 'averageness' that it was even immortalised in a Monty Python's Flying Circus sketch, broadcast on the BBC in 1972. Here, a tourist, Mr Smoke-Too-Much rants to travel agent Mr Bounder about his experiences on package holidays, making frequent references to Watney's Red Barrel. ' ... once a week there's an excursion to the Roman ruins, where you can buy cherryade and melted ice cream and bleedin' Watney's Red Barrel ... '

There was no doubt that in 1977 keg was king, yet Jackson dismissed it in his *World Guide* as, 'Hardly a favourite with the knowing drinker ... '. There was, however, a glimmer of hope for that knowing drinker. In his introduction Jackson wrote, 'In both Germany and Britain, traditional styles of brewing are gaining ground. Sales of *Berliner Weisse* and *Süddeutsche Weizenbier* are on the increase in Germany; so are those of naturally-conditioned *bitter ale* in Britain. Beer is at one and the same time becoming more local and more international.'

The fight back had begun.

Initially, it was modest, paralleling the situation in the USA, where the 1970s and 1980s saw the emergence of a 'craft brewing' movement. A few brave souls set up small-scale, cask-ale brewing operations to bolster the dwindling ranks of established, regional survivors, who kept the flame of cask ale alive during the 'dark days.' One such newcomer was Ringwood Brewery, established in 1978 in a small, former bakery in Hampshire. From very modest beginnings, Ringwood grew to brew more than 30,000 barrels a year. Ironically, its very success caught up with it, and in July 2007 the company was acquired for £19 million by Marston's, described in CAMRA's *Good Beer Guide 2008* as one of three 'New Nationals' on the British brewing scene.

The development of small-scale beer-making enterprises reached its height during the 1990s and earliest years of the 21st century, thanks, in part to supportive government legislation. The *Good Beer Guide 1997* listed no fewer than 68 new breweries, established since the previous edition had gone to press. One significant piece of legislation was popularly known as the 'Beer Orders,' put in place as a result of the Monopolies and Mergers Commission report *The Supply of Beer*, published in 1989. As a result of this report, major brewers were forced to sell off some of their estate of tied houses.[1] No estate was to comprise more than 2,000 pubs, leaving the major firms with many thousands of outlets to divest themselves of within a stipulated three-year period, leading to the rise of what are often termed 'pubcos,' as featured below.

Another well-meaning provision of the 'Beer Orders' was the requirement that a 'guest ale' must be permitted by tenants of licensed premises. This was important for the British independent brewing sector as it stimulated the development of more small-scale ventures, and the number of UK micro-breweries rose from 140 in 1989 to just under 400 in 2001.

However, the anticipated rise in percentage sales of beers turned out by these micro-breweries did not occur, partly due to the fact that tenants often failed to exercise the option of offering a guest ale and partly because the major brewers sold off thousands of pubs to companies not covered by the legislation. The result was a sector which remained static in terms of volume, yet boasted many more producers. Inevitably, the cake came to be cut more thinly.

Progressive Beer Duty was a concept also intended to aid small, independent brewers. The premise of 'PBD,' which originated in Bavaria, is that smaller brewers pay less tax on their products. Introduced into the UK in June 2002, brewers who produced up to 18,330 barrels a year qualified for a sliding rate of tax breaks. The original threshold was subsequently doubled to 36,660 barrels in the March 2004 budget.

The Society of Independent Brewers (SIBA) campaigned long and hard for the introduction of PBD, and SIBA claimed that as a result of its introduction an extra 1,000 jobs had been created in local brewing in the UK by 2005, with 70% of members taking on new staff, while 100 additional breweries joined the organisation. In that year SIBA chairman Keith Bott noted that, 'Anecdotal feedback from members of their investment in expanded capacity suggested they were taking on new staff, but the confirmation of 1,000 jobs created is great news.'

'Progressive Beer Duty helped to give us the kick-start but now there appears to be a virtuous circle. Despite some very tough trading conditions local breweries are reinvesting the benefits of continued sales growth in ensuring they can continue to satisfy and indeed fuel that growth. Local brewing seems to be the brightest light in the UK brewing scene.'

To gain an insight into the current status of British brewing, large and small, it is instructive to look at the data collated by CAMRA for its *Good Beer Guide 2008*. The comparatively risky nature of many independent brewing operations means that between the publication of the 2007 and 2008 guides 23 breweries ceased trading or merged with other operations, but the opposite side of the coin is that the 2008 edition notes 20 new breweries due to be operational during 2007/2008.

In 2007 there were some 640 independent British brewing companies in existence, plus three of what are termed 'New Nationals,' including Greene King plc, owner of the Greene King Brewery in Bury St Edmunds and Belhaven Brewery in Dunbar, plus an estate of some 3,000 pubs. Many of those were acquired due to a policy of taking over and closing regional breweries such as Ridleys and Hardys & Hansons, while maintaining their estates of licensed premises.

A second 'New National' brewer is Marston, Thompson & Evershed, which owns Marston's brewery in Burton upon Trent, Banks & Hansons brewery in Wolverhampton and Jennings in Cockermouth, Cumbria, plus an estate of some 2,500 pubs. Thirdly, the *Good Beer Guide* lists under 'New Nationals' Wells & Young's, based in Bedford, and an amalgamation of the historic Young's of Wandsworth and Charles Wells Ltd.

Finally, the *Good Beer Guide* deals with what it terms 'Global Giants,' reflecting the relative pecking order of importance as far as CAMRA members are concerned! When the most recent guide went to press, eight out of every ten pints of beer consumed in the UK were made by five companies: Anheuser-Busch UK (which brews Budweiser at the former Watney's brewery in Mortlake,

Surrey), Carlsberg UK (operators of the historic Tetley's brewery in Leeds), Coors (which runs the former Bass brewery in Burton), InBev UK and Scottish & Newcastle UK.

However, since publication, Edinburgh-based Scottish & Newcastle, Britain's largest brewer, has been acquired by European rivals Heineken and Carlsberg, while InBev has been taken over by Anheuser-Busch. And so the consolidation process, on a truly global scale, continues.

Looking at the above listing of brewers inevitably begs the question ... just what happened to the 'Big Six' or 'Big Seven' British brewers?'

A significant development of the last two decades has been the retreat of many large brewing companies from 'vertically integrated' operations in which breweries serve a core market of managed or tenanted public houses. Great, historic names like Bass and Whitbread, as well as a host of regional brewers such as Greenall Whitley & Co Ltd in the north-west of England have abandoned brewing entirely in order to operate estates of pubs and other leisure enterprises. Their beers and lagers are now brewed for them under contract by third parties, allowing cost savings and greater flexibility, but at the same time destroying the historic links between brewers, brands and localities.

This has led to the rise of what CAMRA terms 'Pub Groups,' often known as 'pubcos,' which have now replaced brewers as the most important retailers of beer in Britain. The three largest pubcos are Enterprise, Mitchells & Butler and Punch, and most of the pubco chains buy in bulk from brewers to ensure maximum discounts, meaning that there is little diversity and/or regionalisation in the beers they stock.

Yet diversity and regionalisation have gradually been restored to the British brewing scene during the last three decades. The many small-scale, flexible, independent and entrepreneurial operations that have burgeoned have been perfectly placed to be experimental and innovative, developing new beer styles, adapting those of other countries, and reviving old types of beer, widely abandoned or marginalised by the major players. The appearance of many seasonal and 'occasional' beers, principally sold on draught, also adds to the variety of experience available to the drinker.

Such ventures have not only satisfied the creative talents of brewers who in some cases were new to the trade, or in others had 'jumped ship' from major brewers, but also helped give their breweries points of differentiation from their rivals in an increasingly crowded marketplace.

Among the neglected styles of beer that have found new champions among the ranks of independent brewers is 'mild,' dark brown in colour due to the use of well roasted malts or malted barley, and usually quite low in strength. Mild has its origins in the 18th century, but in more recent years the genre was largely abandoned by the major brewers as sales volumes were considered too small to be viable.

Another revived style is 'old ale,' based on the ancient practice of storing ale for months in wooden tuns, producing a style not surprisingly known as 'stale.' It was a key component of porter, and modern interpretations of old ales, usually weaker than in former days, are often matured in the bottle rather than in wooden vessels. Thomas Hardy's Ale is a collectable classic of the genre.

A third revivalist is 'barley wine,' a kind of strong beer that can be stored for lengthy periods, and was originally designed to replace claret at the tables of the great and the good of British society during times of war with France, when the consumption of claret was frowned upon. Modern variants are usually less strong than the originals, which were often as high as 12%abv.

Perhaps the most important style to have seen a reversal in its fortunes is 'porter,' originally a blend of brown ale, pale ale and 'stale' ale. The strongest versions of this mixture were known as stout porter, which was eventually shortened to stout. Most famous is the Irish interpretation, made with the use of a proportion of unmalted roast barley, and termed Dry Irish stout. Modern UK interpretations of stout and porter tend to be closer to the original British type, though reduced in alcoholic strength.

British niche beers such as St Peter's Spiced Ale, from St Peter's Brewery in Suffolk, brewed using cinnamon and apple, are also modern takes on ancient recipes, and some of the most arcane restorations have come courtesy of Williams Brothers Brewing Co, based in the former Scottish brewing capital of Alloa. Bruce and Scott Williams have harnessed indigenous Scottish ingredients to the creation of their beers, the best known being their heather ale, Fraoch, originally brewed many centuries ago in Scotland. Other beers produced to modern versions of old Scottish recipes are flavoured with gooseberries (Grozet ale), Scots Pine (Alba ale) and even seaweed (Kelpie ale).

The most influential continental beer type to have gained favour with UK brewers is wheat beer, a top-fermented style which is made, as the name implies, with a significant quantity of wheat in the recipe, and on Glasgow Green an authentic German brewery has been established in the shape of West Brewing. It is run by Munich-trained brewers who produce a range of continental-style beers in accordance with the ancient German 'purity law' of Reinheitsgebot, using imported German malt, hops and yeast.

Additionally, a number of brewers have also set out to create more characterful 'real' lagers, and the 'real ale revolution' has spawned a new style of ale produced by independent brewers, known as 'golden ale.' It is pale in colour, hoppy, thirst-quenching, quite low in alcohol content, and designed to appeal to mainstream lager drinkers.

Consumers have seen a growing number of beers brewed with the addition of honey, too, and this practice is now common to brewers in many countries around the world. The highest-profile UK 'honey beers' are produced by the leading independents Fuller's (Organic Honey Dew) and Well's (Waggledance).

Typical of the new breed of youthful, entrepreneurial British micro-brewing operations turning out some very innovative beers is BrewDog, based in the Scottish east coast port of Fraserburgh. The story of co-founder Martin Dickie is a familiar one in the micro-brewing business, with Dickie working as brewer for a major English brewing concern before disillusion with 'mass production' methods led him back to his home town and a partnership with old friend James Watt.

BrewDog takes a notably irreverent approach to the whole

business of beer, though at the heart of its philosophy is an insistence on excellence of raw materials and production procedures. BrewDog was established in 2006 and was soon making headlines with its radical fusion of whisky and beer, maturing imperial stout in casks that had formerly held Islay single malt whisky.

Subsequently, BrewDog launched Tokyo, a limited edition, 12% abv stout aged for a month with oak chips and erroneously referred to in some quarters as the UK's strongest beer. This caused controversy with health lobbyists, despite the brewers' robust defence that ' … this is a very expensive, niche beer. For the price of two bottles of Tokyo you can walk into a supermarket and buy a 24-pack of special offer, industrially brewed lager. I know which is more likely to be abused.'

However, naming another beer Speedball, after the heroin-based cocktail associated with the death of actor River Phoenix clearly demonstrates that Messrs Dickie and Watt are comfortable with their role as brewing mavericks!

Two significant and more mainstream developments on the British brewing scene in recent years have been the growing number of organic and bottle-conditioned beers being produced. The popularity of organic beers reflects the increased public interest in all things organic, and even that most traditional of family brewers, Samuel Smith's of Tadcaster in Yorkshire, offers an organic lager.

Bottle-conditioned beers are often referred to as 'real ale in a bottle,' and are the closest it is possible to get to replicating cask ale in bottled format. The beer continues to ferment and mature in the bottle, just as real ale does in a cask while standing in the pub cellar. A number of bottle-conditioned beers are now available in most supermarkets, along with an increasing range of domestic bottled beers of all types, vying with the discounted packs of Stella Artois and Budweiser for shelf space. While this development is a welcome one for consumers and certainly helps to raise the profile of indigenous, independent brewers, the profit margins for producers are notoriously small, and this applies to the major 'international' brewers as much as it does to local 'micro' operations.

Another innovation has been the active targeting of female drinkers by many brewers, no doubt encouraged by Madonna's declaration that she enjoyed a pint of Timothy Taylor's Landlord when she was 'down the boozer' with Guy Ritchie in happier, married times. Coors, the UK's second-largest brewer, has declared its aim of ' … making women love beer as much as they love shoes,' and during the summer of 2008 concocted and promoted a range of beer cocktails, aimed squarely at female consumers.

Some brewers have produced beer formulations that are sweeter and less hoppy in a bid to tempt the ladies' taste buds, while less subtle measures have involved brewing chocolate- and raspberry-flavoured beers. More attractive glassware has also been developed to challenge the dominance of the apparently too masculine straight half-pint or pint glass. Just 12% of UK women drink beer, compared to up to 40% in some European countries, and they obviously represent an enticing, largely untapped market source for brewers and publicans.

The world of beer drinking has also been transformed by the availability of a far wider range of food in pubs than was the case back in the 1970s, when a pickled egg was frequently the only form of sustenance available in male-dominated bars. The growth of food sales has become extremely lucrative and has led to the development of far more family-orientated pubs.

A further step has been taken with the pioneering concept of food and beer pairing, which seeks to elevate the status of beer in Britain by making it a viable alternative to wine as an accompaniment to a meal. A growing number of restaurants offer patrons a 'beer list' in addition to the customary wine list, and the magazine *Beers of the Word* features beer and food pairing articles in each issue.

It might seem reasonable to assume that given so much innovation, entrepreneurial commitment and endeavour that the British beer scene is currently in a comparatively healthy state. Sadly, however, that is far from the truth.

Ironically, at a time when we have a far more numerous and diverse array of British-brewed beers to choose from than we had

30 years ago, the traditions of British drinking have never been under such threat.

Beer sales are declining, partly due to comparatively high levels of taxation, and to take a snapshot of the trends, there was a 4.5% fall in total beer sales during the quarter April to June 2008 compared the same period in 2007, and, even more worryingly, beer sales in pubs fell by 10.6%. Overall, 107 million fewer pints were sold.

Statistically, 1979 is seen as the high point for the UK beer market, with current consumption down a remarkable seven million pints per *day* since that year. UK beer sales in terms of volume are now said to be at their lowest level since the Great Depression of the 1930s.

It is no coincidence that UK wine sales have grown significantly as beer has declined, with sales of wine in Britain rising by 25% between 2001 and 2005 alone. It is estimated that by 2010 UK drinkers will be spending more on wine than the French, Germans or Italians, making Britain the largest retail wine market in Europe. Additionally, there is now a far wider range of 'ready to drink' products and spirits on offer in both the UK on and off-trade sectors, with beer stubbornly continuing to have a down-market, largely male-orientated image, despite the best efforts of the niche brewers and marketers. Furthermore, the vociferous health lobby has doubtless played its part in falling beer sales.

When it comes to the status of the great British pub, the picture becomes even more depressing. For Michael Jackson, the variety and character of local drinking venues was almost as important as the drink itself, whichever country was under discussion. Drink, and the social aspects of drinking, were part of an holistic whole. Back in 1977 when his *World Guide to Beer* was published, the British pub still seemed inviolate. An institution that had evolved through changing times, but seemed secure. However, in 2003 CAMRA claimed 20 pubs were closing each month, which is a worrying statistic in itself, but in July 2008 the same organisation reported that 27 were closing each *week*.

CAMRA spokesman Roy Bray declared, 'Villages become

soulless when the pubs close. There is nowhere left for people to meet and have fun. It is the death of a British institution.'

CAMRA plays a particularly important campaigning role in the fight to save this 'institution,' with its Community Pubs Trust initiative offering support to communities whose pubs are in danger of being lost. Meanwhile, the LocAle campaign encourages pubs to stock beers from local breweries with the aim of reducing their carbon footprints. As delivery costs rise due to spiralling fuel prices this becomes even more attractive for purely economic reasons.

One unusual attempt to involve the local community more actively in the life of a pub and thereby help secure its future concerns the Pigs Pub at Edgefield, near Holt, in Norfolk. There drinkers are being offered the chance to barter home-grown produce in return for free pints of beer. A sign on display in the bar says, 'If you grow, breed, shoot or steal anything that may look at home on our menu, then bring it in and let's do a deal.'

Cleo Wasey, who runs the pub with her business partner and head chef Tim Abbott, says that the scheme has helped to cement the pub's place at the heart of the village community. 'It gives us a more local feel,' she claims.

So just why is the British pub under such threat that extreme measures like these are required?

The reasons are various, with the overall national decline in beer-drinking being one of the more significant, along with the easy availability of inexpensive supermarket beer for home consumption and an increasingly diverse range of wines, not to mention drink-driving legislation and the smoking ban, introduced in 2007.

An additional factor is that there are now many more leisure-time alternatives than there were even 30 years ago, with satellite television and computer-related activities keeping more people than ever indoors, drinking their cheap supermarket purchases. In many cases, too, owners of pubs have found themselves sitting on very lucrative assets, and the temptation to sell to developers who convert the premises, or develop the site for residential use, is often too great to resist.

Alas, the gloom spreads beyond the bar and into the way the heritage of British beer is interpreted and preserved, or more frequently, is not interpreted or preserved. CAMRA runs an admirable campaign designed to safeguard 'at risk' historic pub features, having created a 'National Inventory of Historic Pub Interiors.' This is intended to highlight those aspects of licensed premises that escaped the many, frequently unsympathetic, refurbishments undertaken in the 1960s and 1970s.

However, the problems regarding brewing heritage in Britain are not just confined to the venues in which drinking takes place. Burton upon Trent is the historical centre of British brewing, and is arguably the brewing equivalent to Scotch malt whisky's Speyside or Islay regions, yet its great heritage is now almost entirely uncelebrated.

The former Bass Museum, owned by Coors and rebranded as the Coors Visitor Centre, closed its doors during 2008, with the US-owned company citing falling visitor numbers and running costs of £1 million per year as its reason for calling time on the venture. Yet in Denver, Colorado, Coor's 'brand home' visitor centre attracts in excess of one million people per year. At the time of writing, various rescue plans are being discussed in order to preserve what is undoubtedly an immensely rich and valuable record of British brewing's past.

North of the border, the Scottish Brewing Archive in Glasgow does an admirable job of preservation and interpretation, but its public profile is low and available funds are modest. Access is by appointment only and the archive has a comparatively inconvenient location on the upper floors of a granary in the city's West End.

By contrast, across the country in Edinburgh, the Scotch Whisky Experience just below the castle esplanade welcomes around a quarter of a million people through its doors each year, but the question remains whether a similar enterprise devoted to Scottish brewing would attract anything like the same level of interest. For many visitors, whisky *is* Scotland, as vital a part of their trip as the tourist clichés of haggis, bagpipers and the Loch Ness Monster. But Scottish beer is, perhaps, just beer, and back in

England, Burton upon Trent is hardly the most beguiling tourist hot spot.

There is a clearly a long way to go with beer until we begin to approach the situation pertaining to Scotch whisky, where there seems to be a much greater appreciation of heritage. This may well be, to an extent, because 'heritage' sells whisky, but even if the motives are sometimes cynical, the end result is a positive one. Perhaps it all comes down to the prestige, or lack of it, that beer has in the collective British consciousness.

During his writing career, Michael Jackson worked hard to elevate the prestige of British beer by treating it like the unique and precious drink it really is, appreciating its role in the history and culture of the nation. He was very much part of the movement that took beers back to their roots, in every sense. To borrow a phrase from the poet WH Auden (*Shorts II*) he helped them to become ' … like some valley cheese, local but prized elsewhere.'

For that and for so much else, we should raise a glass of something unpasteurised and uncarbonated to the man who gave us the groundbreaking *Beers of the World.*

NOTES

1 A 'tied house' is a public house, or pub, owned by a brewing company.

CONTRIBUTORS

Carolyn Smagalski

Carolyn is the award-winning editor of Beer and Brewing at BellaOnline, the Voice of Women on the Internet. As the 'Beer Fox,' she has penned over 500 articles and newsletters focused on the craft and on gluten-free beer communities. She contributes to various drinks publications and websites, including Hop Talk, Celebrator, Duvel Moortgat, and de Struise Brouwers.

She is the recipient of the Brewers Association 2006 Beer Journalism Award in Electronic Media for her work at BellaOnline. She co-founded the Annual Philly Beer Geek Competition, is a Certified Beer Judge through the Beer Judge Certification Program, a Certified Beer Server in the Cicerone Certification Program, and is Beer Advisor for the International Gluten-Free Beer Festival. She contributes regularly to the annual Great American Beer Festival in Denver, Colorado, serving as official host and beer-chef at the Beer & Food Pavilion, radio show host on the main stage, and judge in the world's largest commercial beer competition.

Stephen Beaumont

Inspired by Michael Jackson's example, and later strengthened by his friendship, Stephen set out on the path towards becoming a beer writer more than two decades ago. Since then, he has established himself as one of the most authoritative voices on beer

today, as well as a widely recognised writer on spirits, food, cocktails and travel. He is the author or co-author of six books and innumerable articles and columns for publications ranging from *Playboy* to the *Malt Advocate*, epicurious.com to *Wine Enthusiast*, and the *International Herald Tribune* to *Nation's Restaurant News*. Once described as 'beerdom's Brillat-Savarin,' Stephen is nothing if not prolific, vocal and seemingly tireless in his pursuit and endorsement of life's simple liquid pleasures.

Dave Broom

Dave Broom is a Glaswegian writer who gets paid to drink.

Ian Buxton

Ian Buxton is a former Marketing Director of one of Scotland's most famous single malts. He began work in the Scotch whisky industry in 1987; was elected a Keeper of the Quaich in 1991, and holds the Freedom and Livery of the Worshipful Company of Distillers. He is a member of the international tasting panel for the World Whisky Awards and the Scottish Field Merchants' Challenge and is Conference Director of the annual World Whiskies Conference.

He consults widely in the whisky industry; writes regularly for *Whisky Magazine*, the leading UK consumer title, and contributes to a wide variety of other publications. He recently launched www.thewhiskychannel.com, a social networking site for whisky enthusiasts.

Ian has written or co-authored three whisky books and recently completed a new edition of Aeneas MacDonald's 1930 classic *Whisky*. He is currently working on a history of John Dewar & Sons and an account of the reopening of Glenglassaugh Distillery. Ian lives in Perthshire on the site of a former Victorian distillery, Tomdachoille.

John Hansell

John Hansell is an entrepreneur in the whisky industry. He is the founder, publisher and editor of *Malt Advocate*, a magazine for the whisky enthusiast. He also created Whisky Fest, America's

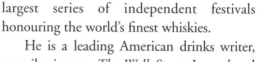

largest series of independent festivals honouring the world's finest whiskies.

He is a leading American drinks writer, contributing to *The Wall Street Journal* and other national media. He lectures and consults regularly on both whisky and beer. He was the first American journalist to be inducted as a Keeper of the Quaich and was also inducted into the Bourbon Hall of Fame for his contributions to the bourbon industry.

Julie Johnson

Julie Johnson is the editor of *All About Beer Magazine*, the oldest American publication for people who love beer. Johnson won the 2007 Beer Journalism Award (Trade and Specialty) – later named the Michael Jackson Beer Journalism Award – from the Brewers' Association. She has had a regular column in the *News and Observer*, and now in the *Independent Weekly*, both based in North Carolina. Johnson has also written for *Cheers*,

Beverage Dynamics, *The Brewers Guardian*, and Smoke. Michael Jackson wrote a regular column for *All About Beer* for 23 years, his longest association with a magazine.

Charles MacLean

Charles MacLean has been researching, writing and lecturing about whisky since 1981. He is the author of ten books on the subject (the most recent is *Whiskypedia*, February 2009), writes regularly about Scotch in several magazines around the world, and hosts a TV channel dedicated to world whiskies at *www.singlemalt.TV*.

Hans Offringa

Hans Offringa is a Dutch author, media expert and whisky connoisseur. He is bilingual and writes in both Dutch and English. His has written three novels, a historical book and a DVD about the raising of the Russian nuclear submarine *Kursk*,

a series of comical drawing books and 10 books on whisky, including *The Road to Craigellachie, The Legend of Laphroaig, A Taste of Whisky* and *Whisky & Jazz*.

Hans translated Michael Jackson's *Whisky: The Definitive Guide* and *The Malt Whisky Companion* into Dutch. He regularly contributes to various whisky magazines and whisky websites and has been producing mini-documentaries for *singlemalt.tv.* since its inception. Together with his American wife Becky he gives whisky presentations in Europe and the USA under the name *The Whisky Couple*. Their website can be found at: www.thewhiskycouple.com.

F Paul Pacult

F Paul Pacult is the founding editor and publisher of *F. Paul Pacult's Spirit Journal – The Quarterly Independent Guide to Distilled Spirits, Beers, and Wines* newsletter now in its 18th year of publication. He is the author of five other critically acclaimed books on beer and spirits.

He contributes widely to a wide range of national journals and the broadcast media in North America. He is the judging director at the annual San Francisco World Spirits Competition and a founding member of Beverage Alcohol Resource LLC (BAR).

He has won many awards for his writing and is a not only a Master of the Quaich, but is also enrolled in The Bourbon Hall of Fame as well as being a member of the Armagnac Company of Musketeers. Paul lives in New York State's Hudson Valley with his wife and partner Sue Woodley.

Roger Protz

Roger Protz is one of the world's leading beer writers. He is the author of 17 books and has edited 18 editions of the annual *Good*

Beer Guide. He travels extensively, a fact underscored by his forthcoming memoirs, *Life on the Hop*. He has twice been named Glenfiddich Drink Writer of the Year and was awarded a Lifetime Achievement Award by the British Guild of Beer Writers. His book *300 Beers To Try Before You Die* is one of the

best-selling books on the subject. He lives in St Albans in Hertfordshire. His only known leisure pursuits are walking the dog (to the pub) and supporting West Ham United FC. His website is www.beer-pages.com

Lucy Saunders

Lucy Saunders is the author of *The Best of American Beer and Food* and editor of beercook.com. She thinks of beer as food.

Michael Jackson encouraged her to start writing about beer, and so she has championed the presence of craft beer at the American table for over 20 years. She now lectures and conducts tasting classes at cooking schools, retailers and non-profit groups, including the Smithsonian. She has

worked with the International Association of Culinary Professionals, the Fancy Food Shows, the American Culinary Federation, and other food trade groups to conduct beer and food pairings. She lives in Milwaukee, Wisconsin, USA.

Conrad Seidl

Conrad Seidl was born in Vienna in 1958 and is known as 'der Bierpapst' ('the pope of beer'). He has worked for daily newspapers and culinary magazines for the past 25 years. He is the editor of the *Austrian Beer Guide* and has authored more than a dozen other books on  beer. He has won several awards including that of best beer writer in the German language in 1993.

Gavin D Smith

Gavin D Smith is one of Scotland's leading drinks writers and contributing editor to www.whisky-pages.com. He is the author  of some 20 books, a dozen of which are on the subject of whisky. He is also author of *The Scottish Beer Bible* (Mercat Press, 2001), *British Brewing in Old Photographs* (Sutton Publishing, 2004) and has contributed to *What's Brewing and Beers of the World*. He lives on the Fife coast in Scotland.

Other titles from Classic Expressions

Currently three limited edition facsimile reprints of whisky classics are available exclusively from www.classicexpressions.co.uk. These have all been produced as 300 numbered copies and are all priced at £50 plus post and packing (dependent on country of destination). As an added bonus each book not only comes in a protective slipcase, but is also accompanied by a *free* CD that has a full read- and search-only file of the book's contents to aid researchers and whisky historians alike.

Joseph Pacy's REMINISCENCES OF A GAUGER is one of the most important works of its period. Pacy spent some 40 years as a 'gauger' or Excise Officer in Scotland and England rising eventually to the rank of Collector in Lincoln.

In 1873, after Pacy's son had died tragically, he published this account of his life and work in an effort to raise funds for his son's widow and four children who had been left destitute by their loss. All profits from the sale of the book went to his daughter-in-law. The book sheds much light, not only on the day-to-day routines of the Excise, but also airs Pacy's often enlightened and controversial thoughts on the organisation of the Excise service and the adverse affects of high rates of duty on free trade.

It also provides a dramatic and, at times, highly personal account of his work at a number of locations round the country. In particular, Pacy worked with the colourful and dogmatic Captain Fraser at Royal Brackla Distillery. His book is the only known contemporary account of Fraser at a time when this distillery (still in production today) was one of the most highly regarded in the whole of Scotland.

> I know that I never encountered a man either in or out of the service that tested my courage, my prudence, or my honesty, more than this same distiller.

Previous to this in Campbeltown he broke a malt fraud ring. The account of this is extremely engaging as his professional duty is weighed up against his understanding of the reasons for the crime:

The difference of the tax on the two kinds of malt was a temptation to attempt to pass barley on the excise for bere and bigg, which, considering the regulations I have alluded to, was not easy to resist.

REMINISCENCES OF A GAUGER exists only in the rare 1873 edition and has never been reprinted. You might expect to pay £250-£300 for a good copy – if you could find one.

Ian MacDonald's SMUGGLING IN THE HIGHLANDS is a seminal volume of whisky history. The author was a highly-regarded and long-serving excise officer, who spent much of his career in the Scottish Highlands where he came to know the people and their whisky-related 'ploys' very well.

MacDonald had a keen eye for a good story, and many of the enthralling anecdotes recounted in the chapter entitled 'Smuggling Stories and Detections' have never subsequently been published.

Despite his ability to tell a good smuggling story, however, there is no doubt that MacDonald had little sympathy with the law breakers whose activities he chronicled. Indeed, it is typical of the man, and his era, that an entire, and wholly fascinating, chapter is devoted to 'Moral Aspects of Smuggling.'

Much of the material in SMUGGLING IN THE HIGHLANDS was first read before the Gaelic Society of Inverness during the late 1880s, at a time when whisky smuggling was resurgent in the north of Scotland. It was subsequently printed in the *Transactions of the Society* and was  published as a series of articles in *The Highlander and Celtic Magazine*. As a book it appeared in 1914, and this facsimile edition is an essential and long-overdue edition for anyone truly interested in the heritage of Scotch whisky and Scottish social life a century and more ago.

There can be no doubt that "good, pious men" engaged in smuggling, and there is less doubt that equally good, pious men – ministers and priests – were grateful recipients of a large share of the smugglers' produce. Some of the old lairds not only winked at the practice, but actively encouraged it.

SMUGGLING IN THE HIGHLANDS was published in 1914. A good, clean copy of the illustrated edition, which our facsimile faithfully reproduces, would cost at least £150.

Our third new title is the exceedingly rare 1st edition of *TRUTHS ABOUT WHISKY*, issued by the four principal Dublin distillers in 1878. As they say in the first chapter:

> The four firms of whisky distillers by whom this book is published ... have for the last two years been engaged in an endeavour to place some check upon the practices of the fraudulent traders by whom silent spirit, variously disguised and flavoured, is sold under the name of Whisky.

Note the spelling of 'whisky', even in Ireland! 'Silent spirit' is, of course, a reference to grain whisky and the book is an impassioned defence of malt whisky. It includes details on 'The Qualities and Popularity of

genuine Dublin Whisky', 'The Growth of Silent Spirit into Sham Whisky', 'Grogging' and 'Whisky Frauds'.

The book is an important contribution to the great 'what is whisky' debate, which was even then gathering pace and culminated in the 1909 Royal Commission, the recommendations of which shaped the future direction of the distilling industry.

As well as being an utterly fascinating insight into late Victorian attitudes, the book contains four wonderful gatefold coloured plates (approx 14" x 8.5") giving a bird's-eye view of the distilleries of the following distilleries as they appeared in 1878: John Jameson & Sons; William Jameson & Co (of Marrowbone Lane); John Power & Sons and George Roe & Co. All gone now, of course.

An original copy of this book recently sold for £750. It is eagerly sought after by whisky collectors and those interested in the history of Dublin, its whisky makers and its distilleries.

To purchase any or all of these unique titles, simply log onto:
www.classicexpressions.co.uk